low cholesterol

step-by-step recipes for a healthier lifestyle

LOW FAT

CHRISTINE FRANCE

low cholesterol
step-by-step recipes for a healthier lifestyle
LOW FAT

HERMES HOUSE

This edition published by Hermes House in 2002

© Anness Publishing Limited 1996, 2002

Published in the USA by Hermes House
Anness Publishing Inc.
27 West 20th Street
New York
NY 10011

Hermes House is an imprint of Anness Publishing Inc.

Publisher: Joanna Lorenz
Senior Cookery Editor: Linda Fraser
Assistant Editor: Emma Brown
Designer: Siân Keogh
Photographers: Karl Adamson, Steve Baxter,
James Duncan, Amanda Heywood and Don Last
Food for Photography: Carla Capalbo, Elizabeth Wolf-Cohen,
Wendy Lee and Jane Stevenson
Props Stylists: Madeleine Brehaut, Blake Minton,
Kirsty Rawlings and Fiona Tillet

Front cover shows Jambalaya. For recipe see page 70
Previously published as *The Ultimate Low Cholesterol Low Fat Cookbook,*

1 3 5 7 9 10 8 6 4 2

NOTES
Standard spoon and cup measures are level.

Large eggs are used unless otherwise stated.

CONTENTS

WHY A LOW FAT DIET?

We need a certain amount of fat in our diet for general health and it is a valuable source of energy. Also, it plays a vital role in making foods palatable to eat. However, most of us eat more fat than we need. You should not try to cut out fat altogether, but a lower fat diet has the benefits of weight loss and reduction in the risk of heart disease.

There are two types of fat – saturated and unsaturated. The unsaturated group includes two types – polyunsaturated and monounsaturated fats.

Saturated fats are the ones you should limit, as they increase cholesterol in the blood, and this can increase the risk of heart disease. The main sources of saturated fat are animal products such as dairy products and meat, but also hard fats and hydrogenated vegetable fat or oil.

Polyunsaturated fats are essential in small quantities for good health, and are thought to help reduce the cholesterol in the blood. There is also some evidence that monounsaturated fats have a beneficial effect. The main sources of polyunsaturates are vegetable oils such as sunflower, corn and soybean, and oily fish such as herring, mackerel, sardines, and trout. Sources of monounsaturated fats include olive and peanut oils, as well as avocados and many nuts.

Cutting Down on Cholesterol?
Cholesterol is a substance which occurs naturally in the blood, and is essential for the formation of hormones, body cells, nerves, and bile salts which help digestion.

A high cholesterol level can increase the likelihood of coronary heart disease, as it becomes deposited on the walls of the arteries, causing them to fur up. The main cause of raised cholesterol levels is eating too much fat, especially saturated fat. Eating too much saturated fat encourages the body to make more cholesterol than it needs, and also seems to prevent it getting rid of the excess.

The cholesterol found in foods such as egg yolk, liver, cheese, butter, and shellfish does not have a major effect on the amount of blood cholesterol in most people, but it is best not to eat large quantities of these foods too often.

Fresh approach: when you are shopping for low fat foods, choose fresh seasonal vegetables (top right) and cook them without added fat. Salads (right) are a good accompaniment too, just use a polyunsaturated or monounsaturated oil for the dressing. Fresh fruits (above) are the perfect ending to a low fat meal if you haven't time to cook – eat them either raw in a salad or poach in fruit juice and serve hot with yogurt.

EASY WAYS TO CUT DOWN FAT AND SATURATED FAT

EAT LESS	TRY INSTEAD
Butter and hard fats.	Try spreading butter more thinly, or replace it with a low fat spread or polyunsaturated margarine.
Fatty meats and high-fat products such as meat dishes in heavy sauces and sausages.	Buy the leanest cuts of meat you can find and choose low fat meats like skinless chicken or turkey. Look for reduced-fat sausages and meat products. Eat fish more often, especially oily fish.
Full-fat dairy products like cream, butter, yogurt, milk, and hard cheeses.	Choose skimmed or semi-skimmed milk and milk products, and try low fat yogurt, low fat fromage frais, and lower fat cheeses such as skim milk cream cheese, reduced fat Cheddar, mozzarella, or Brie.
Cooking fats such as lard or shortening.	Choose polyunsaturated oils for cooking, such as olive, sunflower, corn, or soybean oil.
Rich salad dressings like Blue Cheese or Thousand Island.	Make salad dressings with low fat yogurt or fromage frais, or use a healthy oil such as olive oil.
Fried foods.	Broil, microwave, steam, or bake when possible. Roast meats on a rack. Fill up on starchy foods like pasta, rice, and couscous. Choose baked or boiled potatoes, not fries.
Added fat in cooking.	Use heavy-based or nonstick pans so you can cook with little or no added fat.
High fat snacks such as chips, chocolate, cakes, pastries, and cookies.	Choose fresh or dried fruit, breadsticks, or vegetable sticks. Make your own low fat cakes and baked goods.

APPETIZERS AND SNACKS

For a healthy diet it makes good sense to include some home-made soups in everyday meals, packed with the goodness of fresh ingredients and very low in fat. As a light lunch with crusty bread, or as an appetizer, modern soups are extremely quick and easy to make. The Thai-style Corn Soup takes only two to three minutes. An added bonus is the variety of fresh, seasonal vegetables available all year. Other appetizers can double up as a light meal or snack. It pays to have a selection of these healthy, quick snack foods handy. For simple snacks or lunch boxes, pitas, whole-wheat rolls, or tacos can contain a tasty, low fat filling like chili-spiced tuna salad. Some snacks are elegant enough for dinner party appetizers too.

CAULIFLOWER AND WALNUT CREAM

Even though there's no cream added to this soup, the cauliflower gives it a delicious, rich, creamy texture.

INGREDIENTS

Serves 4
1 medium cauliflower
1 medium onion, coarsely chopped
1⅞ cups chicken or vegetable
    broth
1⅞ cups skim milk
3 tbsp walnut pieces
salt and black pepper
paprika and chopped walnuts, to
    garnish

1 Trim the cauliflower of outer leaves and break into small florets. Place the cauliflower, onion, and broth in a large saucepan.

2 Bring to a boil, cover, and simmer for about 15 minutes, or until soft. Add the milk and walnuts, then purée in a food processor until smooth.

3 Season the soup to taste, then bring to a boil. Serve sprinkled with paprika and chopped walnuts.

NUTRITION NOTES

Per portion:
Energy	166Kcals/699kJ
Fat	9.02g
Saturated fat	0.88g
Cholesterol	2.25mg
Fiber	2.73g

CURRIED CARROT AND APPLE SOUP

INGREDIENTS

Serves 4
2 tsp sunflower oil
1 tbsp mild curry powder
1¼ lb carrots, chopped
1 large onion, chopped
1 tart baking apple, chopped
3⅔ cups chicken broth
salt and black pepper
plain low fat yogurt and carrot curls, to
    garnish

NUTRITION NOTES

Per portion:
Energy	114Kcals/477kJ
Fat	3.57g
Saturated fat	0.43g
Cholesterol	0.4mg
Fiber	4.99g

1 Heat the oil and gently fry the curry powder for 2–3 minutes.

2 Add the carrots, onion, and apple, stir well, then cover the pan.

3 Cook over very low heat for about 15 minutes, shaking the pan occasionally until softened. Spoon the vegetable mixture into a food processor or blender, then add half the broth and process until smooth.

4 Return to the pan and pour in the remaining broth. Bring the soup to a boil and adjust the seasoning before serving in bowls, garnished with a swirl of yogurt and a few curls of carrot.

SPLIT PEA AND ZUCCHINI SOUP

Rich and satisfying, this tasty and nutritious soup will warm a chilly winter's day.

INGREDIENTS

Serves 4

1⅞ cups yellow split peas
1 medium onion, finely chopped
1 tsp sunflower oil
2 medium zucchini, finely diced
3¾ cups chicken broth
½ tsp ground turmeric
salt and black pepper

1 Place the split peas in a bowl, cover with cold water, and leave to soak for several hours or overnight. Drain, rinse in cold water, and drain again.

2 Cook the onion in the oil in a covered pan, shaking occasionally, until soft. Reserve a handful of diced zucchini and add the rest to the pan. Cook, stirring, for 2–3 minutes.

3 Add the broth and turmeric to the pan and bring to a boil. Reduce the heat, then cover and simmer for 30–40 minutes, or until the split peas are tender. Adjust the seasoning.

4 When the soup is almost ready, bring a large saucepan of water to a boil, add the reserved diced zucchini, and cook for 1 minute, then drain and add to the soup before serving hot with warm crusty bread.

COOK'S TIP
For a quicker alternative, use split red lentils for this soup – they need no pre-soaking and cook very quickly. Adjust the amount of broth, if necessary.

NUTRITION NOTES

Per portion:	
Energy	174Kcals/730kJ
Fat	2.14g
Saturated fat	0.54g
Cholesterol	0
Fiber	3.43g

RED BELL PEPPER SOUP WITH LIME

The beautiful rich red color of this soup makes it a very attractive appetizer or light lunch. For a special dinner, toast some tiny croutons and serve sprinkled into the soup.

INGREDIENTS

Serves 4–6
4 red bell peppers, seeded and chopped
1 large onion, chopped
1 tsp olive oil
1 garlic clove, crushed
1 small red chili, sliced
3 tbsp tomato paste
3¾ cups chicken broth
finely grated rind and juice of 1 lime
salt and black pepper
shreds of lime rind, to garnish

1 Cook the onion and bell peppers gently in the oil in a covered saucepan for about 5 minutes, shaking the pan occasionally, until softened.

2 Stir in the garlic, then add the chili with the tomato paste. Stir in half the broth, then bring to a boil. Cover the pan and simmer for 10 minutes.

3 Cool slightly, then purée in a food processor or blender. Return to the pan, then add the remaining broth, the lime rind and juice, and seasoning.

4 Bring the soup back to a boil, then serve at once with a few strips of lime rind, scattered into each bowl.

NUTRITION NOTES	
Per portion:	
Energy	87Kcals/366kJ
Fat	1.57g
Saturated fat	0.12g
Cholesterol	0
Fiber	3.40g

BEET AND APRICOT SWIRL

This soup is most attractive if you swirl together the two colored mixtures, but if you prefer they can be mixed together to save on time and dishes.

INGREDIENTS

Serves 4

4 large cooked beets, coarsely chopped
1 small onion, coarsely chopped
2½ cups chicken broth
1 cup dried apricots
1 cup orange juice
salt and black pepper

1 Place the beets and half the onion in a pan with the broth. Bring to a boil, then reduce the heat, cover, and simmer for about 10 minutes. Purée in a food processor or blender.

2 Place the rest of the onion in a pan with the apricots and orange juice, cover, and simmer gently for about 15 minutes, until tender. Purée in a food processor or blender.

3 Return the two mixtures to the saucepans and reheat. Season to taste with salt and pepper, then swirl them together in individual soup bowls for a marbled effect.

COOK'S TIP
The apricot mixture should be the same consistency as the beet mixture – if it is too thick, then add a little more orange juice.

NUTRITION NOTES

Per portion:

Energy	135Kcals/569kJ
Fat	0.51g
Saturated fat	0.01g
Cholesterol	0
Fiber	4.43g

THAI-STYLE CORN SOUP

This is a very quick and easy soup, made in minutes. If you are using frozen shrimp, then defrost them first before adding to the soup.

INGREDIENTS

Serves 4

½ tsp sesame or sunflower oil
2 scallions, thinly sliced
1 garlic clove, crushed
2½ cups chicken broth
15oz can cream-style corn
1¼ cups cooked, peeled
   shrimp
1 tsp green chili paste or chili sauce
   (optional)
salt and black pepper
fresh cilantro leaves, to garnish

1 Heat the oil in a large heavy-based saucepan and sauté the scallions and garlic over medium heat for 1 minute, until softened, but not browned.

2 Stir in the chicken broth, cream-style corn, shrimp, and chili paste or sauce, if using.

3 Bring the soup to a boil, stirring occasionally. Season to taste, then serve at once, sprinkled with fresh cilantro leaves to garnish.

COOK'S TIP
If cream-style corn is not available, use ordinary canned corn, puréed in a food processor for a few seconds, until creamy yet with some texture left.

NUTRITION NOTES

Per portion:

Energy	202Kcals/848kJ
Fat	3.01g
Saturated fat	0.43g
Cholesterol	45.56mg
Fiber	1.6g

MEDITERRANEAN TOMATO SOUP

Children will love this soup – especially if you use fancy shapes of pasta such as alphabet or animal shapes.

INGREDIENTS

Serves 4

1½ lb ripe plum tomatoes
1 medium onion, quartered
1 celery stalk
1 garlic clove
1 tbsp olive oil
1⅞ cups chicken broth
2 tbsp tomato paste
½ cup small pasta shapes
salt and black pepper
fresh cilantro or parsley, to garnish

1 Place the tomatoes, onion, celery, and garlic in a pan with the oil. Cover and cook over low heat for 40–45 minutes, shaking the pan occasionally, until very soft.

2 Spoon the vegetables into a food processor or blender and process until smooth. Press through a strainer, then return to the pan.

3 Stir in the broth and tomato paste and bring to a boil. Add the pasta and simmer gently for about 8 minutes, or until the pasta is tender. Add salt and pepper to taste, then sprinkle with cilantro or parsley and serve hot.

NUTRITION NOTES

Per portion:

Energy	112Kcals/474kJ
Fat	3.61g
Saturated fat	0.49g
Cholesterol	0
Fiber	2.68g

MUSHROOM, CELERY, AND GARLIC SOUP

INGREDIENTS

Serves 4

3 cups chopped mushrooms
4 celery stalks, chopped
3 garlic cloves
3 tbsp dry sherry or white wine
3⅔ cups chicken broth
2 tbsp Worcestershire sauce
1 tsp ground nutmeg
salt and black pepper
celery leaves, to garnish

NUTRITION NOTES

Per portion:

Energy	48Kcals/200kJ
Fat	1.09g
Saturated fat	0.11g
Cholesterol	0
Fiber	1.64g

1 Place the mushrooms, celery, and garlic in a pan and stir in the sherry or wine. Cover and cook over low heat for 30–40 minutes, until tender.

2 Add half the broth and purée in a food processor or blender until smooth. Return to the pan and add the remaining broth, the Worcestershire sauce, and nutmeg.

3 Bring to a boil, season, and serve hot, garnished with celery leaves.

TOMATO AND CILANTRO SOUP

This delicious soup is an ideal solution when time is short but you still want to produce a very stylish appetizer.

INGREDIENTS

Serves 4

1½lb small fresh tomatoes
2 tbsp vegetable oil
1 bay leaf
4 scallions, cut into
   1in pieces
1 tsp salt
1 garlic clove, crushed
1 tsp crushed black
   peppercorns
2 tbsp chopped fresh cilantro
3 cups water
1 tbsp cornstarch
4 tbsp single cream,
   to garnish

1 To skin the tomatoes, plunge them into very hot water for 30 seconds, then transfer to a bowl of cold water. The skin should now peel off quickly and easily. Chop the tomatoes into large chunks.

2 Heat the oil in a large saucepan, add the bay leaf and scallions, then stir in the tomatoes. Cook, stirring for a few more minutes until the tomatoes are softened.

3 Add the salt, garlic, peppercorns, cilantro and water, bring to a boil, then simmer for 15 minutes.

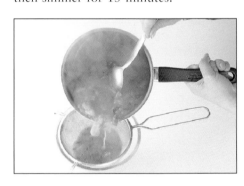

4 Dissolve the cornstarch in a little water, remove the soup from the heat and press through a strainer.

5 Return the soup to the pan, add the cornstarch mixture and stir over a gentle heat until boiling and thickened.

6 Ladle the soup into shallow soup plates, then swirl a tablespoon of cream into each bowl before serving.

NUTRITION NOTES

Per portion:
Energy	113Kcals/474kJ
Fat	7.16g
Saturated fat	1.37g
Cholesterol	2.8mg

BUCKWHEAT BLINIS

INGREDIENTS

Serves 4

1 tsp fast-rising dried yeast
1 cup skim milk
⅓ cup buckwheat flour
⅓ cup flour
2 tsp sugar
pinch of salt
1 egg, separated
lamb's lettuce, to serve

For the avocado cream
1 large avocado
⅓ cup low fat ricotta cheese
juice of 1 lime
cracked black peppercorns,
* to garnish*

For the pickled beets
8oz beets, peeled
3 tbsp lime juice
snipped fresh chives, to garnish

1 Mix the dried yeast with the milk, then mix with the flours, sugar, pinch of salt and egg yolk. Cover with a dish towel and leave to prove for about 40 minutes. Then whisk the egg white until stiff but not dry and fold into the blini mixture.

2 Heat a little oil in a nonstick frying pan and add a ladleful of batter to make a 4in pancake. Cook for about 2–3 minutes on each side. Repeat with the remaining batter mixture to make eight blinis.

3 For the avocado cream, cut the avocado in half and remove the pit. Peel and place the flesh in a food processor or blender with the ricotta cheese and lime juice. Process until the mixture is very smooth.

4 For the pickle, shred the beets finely. Mix with the lime juice. To serve, top each blini with a spoonful of avocado cream and garnish with cracked peppercorns. Serve with lamb's lettuce and the pickled beets, garnished with chives.

NUTRITION NOTES

Per portion:

Energy	304Kcals/1277kJ
Fat	16.56g
Saturated fat	2.23g
Cholesterol	56.3mg
Fiber	3.3g

COOK'S TIP
Serve with a glass of chilled vodka for a special occasion.

Eggplant and Garlic Pâté

Serve this garlicky pâté of smoky baked eggplant and red bell peppers on a bed of salad, accompanied by crispbreads.

Ingredients

Serves 4

3 eggplants
2 red bell peppers
5 garlic cloves
1½ tsp pink peppercorns in brine,
*   drained and crushed*
2 tbsp chopped fresh cilantro,
*   or parsley*

Nutrition Notes

Per portion:

Energy	70Kcals/292kJ
Fat	1.32g
Saturated fat	0
Cholesterol	0
Fiber	5.96g

1 Preheat the oven to 400°F. Arrange the whole eggplants, bell peppers and garlic cloves on a baking sheet and place in the oven. After 10 minutes remove the garlic cloves, and turn over the eggplants and bell peppers. Return the baking sheet to the oven.

2 Carefully peel the garlic cloves and place in the bowl of a food processor or blender.

3 After 20 minutes more remove the blistered and charred bell peppers from the oven and place in a plastic bag. Leave to cool.

4 After 10 minutes more remove the eggplants from the oven. Split in half and scoop the flesh into a strainer placed over a bowl. Press the flesh with a spoon to remove the bitter juices.

5 Add the eggplant flesh to the garlic in the food processor or blender, and process until smooth. Place in a large mixing bowl.

6 Peel and chop the bell peppers and stir into the eggplant mixture. Mix in the peppercorns and fresh cilantro or parsley, and serve at once.

CUCUMBER AND ALFALFA TORTILLAS

Wheat tortillas are extremely simple to prepare at home. Served with a crisp, fresh salsa, they make a marvelous appetizer, light lunch or supper dish.

INGREDIENTS

Serves 4
2 cups flour, sifted
pinch of salt
3 tbsp olive oil
½–⅔ cup warm water
lime wedges, to garnish

For the salsa
1 red onion, finely chopped
1 red chili, seeded and
  finely chopped
2 tbsp chopped fresh dill
  or cilantro
½ cucumber, peeled and chopped
2 cups alfalfa sprouts

For the sauce
1 large ripe avocado, peeled
  and pitted
juice of 1 lime
2 tbsp soft goat cheese
pinch of paprika

1 Mix all the salsa ingredients together in a bowl and set aside.

2 For the sauce, place the avocado, lime juice and goat cheese in a food processor or blender and process until smooth. Place in a bowl and cover with plastic wrap. Dust with paprika just before serving.

3 For the tortillas, place the flour and salt in a food processor or blender, add the oil and process. Gradually add the water until a stiff dough has formed. Turn out on to a floured board and knead until smooth.

4 Divide the mixture into eight pieces. Knead each piece for a couple of minutes and form into a ball. Flatten and roll out each ball to a 9in round.

NUTRITION NOTES

Per portion:

Energy	395Kcals/1659kJ
Fat	20.17g
Saturated fat	1.69g
Cholesterol	4.38mg
Fiber	4.15g

5 Heat a nonstick or ungreased heavy-based pan. Cook one tortilla at a time for about 30 seconds on each side. Place the cooked tortillas in a clean dish towel and repeat until you have made eight tortillas.

6 Spread each tortilla with a spoonful of avocado sauce, top with the salsa and roll up. Serve garnished with lime wedges and eat immediately.

COOK'S TIP
When peeling the avocado be sure to scrape off the bright green flesh from immediately under the skin as this gives the sauce its vivid green color.

CHEESE AND SPINACH PUFFS

INGREDIENTS

Serves 6

1 cup cooked, chopped spinach
¾ cup cottage cheese
1 tsp ground nutmeg
2 egg whites
2 tbsp grated Parmesan cheese
salt and black pepper

1 Preheat the oven to 425°F. Brush six ramekin dishes with oil.

2 Mix together the spinach and cottage cheese in a small bowl, then add the nutmeg and seasoning to taste.

3 Whisk the egg whites in a separate bowl until stiff enough to hold soft peaks. Fold them evenly into the spinach mixture using a spatula or large metal spoon, then spoon the mixture into the oiled ramekins, dividing it evenly, and smooth the tops.

4 Sprinkle with the Parmesan and place on a baking sheet. Bake for 15–20 minutes, or until puffed and golden brown. Serve immediately.

NUTRITION NOTES

Per portion:
Energy	47Kcals/195kJ
Fat	1.32g
Saturated fat	0.52g
Cholesterol	2.79mg
Fiber	0.53g

LEMONY STUFFED ZUCCHINI

INGREDIENTS

Serves 4

4 zucchini, about 6oz each
1 tsp sunflower oil
1 garlic clove, crushed
1 tsp ground lemongrass
finely grated rind and juice of ½ lemon
scant ¾ cup cooked long-grain rice
6oz cherry tomatoes, halved
2 tbsp toasted cashews
salt and black pepper
sprigs of thyme, to garnish

NUTRITION NOTES

Per portion:
Energy	126Kcals/530kJ
Fat	5.33g
Saturated fat	0.65g
Cholesterol	0
Fiber	2.31g

1 Preheat the oven to 400°F. Halve the zucchini lengthwise and use a teaspoon to scoop out the centers. Blanch the shells in boiling water for 1 minute, then drain well.

2 Chop the zucchini flesh finely and place in a saucepan with the oil and garlic. Stir over moderate heat until softened, but not browned.

3 Stir in the lemongrass, lemon rind and juice, rice, tomatoes, and cashews. Season well and spoon into the zucchini shells. Place the shells in a baking pan and cover with foil.

4 Bake for 25–30 minutes or until the zucchini is tender, then serve hot, garnished with thyme sprigs.

CHINESE GARLIC MUSHROOMS

Tofu is high in protein and very low in fat, so it is a very useful food to keep handy for quick meals and snacks like this one.

INGREDIENTS

Serves 4

8 large open cup mushrooms
3 scallions, sliced
1 garlic clove, crushed
2 tbsp oyster sauce
10oz packet marinated tofu, cut into small dice
7oz can corn, drained
2 tsp sesame oil
salt and black pepper

1 Preheat the oven to 400°F. Finely chop the mushroom stalks and mix with the scallions, garlic, and oyster sauce.

2 Stir in the diced marinated tofu and corn, season well with salt and pepper, then carefully spoon the filling into the mushrooms.

3 Brush the edges of the mushrooms with the sesame oil. Arrange the stuffed mushrooms in a baking dish and bake for 12–15 minutes, until the mushrooms are just tender, then serve at once.

COOK'S TIP
If you prefer, omit the oyster sauce and use light soy sauce instead.

NUTRITION NOTES

Per portion:

Energy	137Kcals/575kJ
Fat	5.6g
Saturated fat	0.85g
Cholesterol	0
Fiber	1.96g

SURPRISE SCOTCH 'EGGS'

This reduced fat version of Scotch eggs is great for lunch boxes or picnics. If half-fat sausage meat isn't available, buy half-fat sausages or turkey sausages and remove the skins.

INGREDIENTS

Makes 3

*5 tbsp chopped parsley and snipped
  chives, mixed
½ cup low fat cream
  cheese
1 lb half fat sausage meat
½ cup oatmeal
salt and black pepper
lettuce and tomato salad, to serve*

1 Preheat the oven to 400°F. Mix together the herbs, cheese, and seasonings, then roll into three even-sized balls.

2 Divide the sausage meat into thirds and press each piece out to a round, about ½ in thick.

3 Wrap each cheese ball in a piece of sausage meat, smoothing all over to enclose the cheese completely. Spread out the oatmeal on a plate and roll the balls in the oatmeal, using your hands to coat them evenly.

4 Place the balls on a baking sheet and bake for 30–35 minutes or until golden. Serve hot or cold, with a lettuce and tomato salad.

NUTRITION NOTES

Per portion:

Energy	352Kcals/1476kJ
Fat	15.94g
Saturated fat	0.29g
Cholesterol	66.38mg
Fiber	3.82g

CHICKEN NAAN POCKETS

INGREDIENTS

Serves 4

4 small naan
3 tbsp plain low fat yogurt
1½ tsp garam masala
1 tsp chili powder
1 tsp salt
3 tbsp lemon juice
1 tbsp chopped fresh cilantro
1 green chili, chopped
1lb chicken without skin and
*   bone, cubed*
1 tbsp sunflower oil (optional)
8 onion rings
2 tomatoes, quartered
½ white cabbage, shredded

For the garnish
lemon wedges
2 small tomatoes, halved
mixed salad leaves
fresh cilantro leaves

1 Cut into the middle of each naan to make a pocket, then set aside.

2 Mix together the yogurt, garam masala, chili powder, salt, lemon juice, fresh cilantro and chopped green chili. Pour the marinade over the chopped chicken and leave to marinate for about 1 hour.

3 After 1 hour preheat the broiler to very hot, then lower the heat to medium. Place the chicken in a flameproof dish and broil for about 15–20 minutes until tender and cooked through, turning the chicken pieces at least twice. Baste with the oil while cooking if required.

COOK'S TIP
Use ready-made naans available in some supermarkets and Asian stores for speed.

4 Remove from the heat and fill each naan with the chicken and then with the onion rings, tomatoes and cabbage. Serve with the garnish ingredients immediately.

NUTRITION NOTES
Per portion:
Energy	364Kcals/1529kJ
Fat	10.85g
Saturated fat	3.01g
Cholesterol	65.64mg

CHICKEN TIKKA

INGREDIENTS

Serves 6

1lb chicken without skin and bone,
*   chopped or cubed*
1in piece fresh ginger root, chopped
1 garlic clove, crushed
1 tsp chili powder
¼ tsp turmeric
1 tsp salt
⅔ cup plain low fat yogurt
4 tbsp lemon juice
1 tbsp chopped fresh cilantro
1 tbsp sunflower oil

For the garnish
1 small onion, cut into rings
lime wedges
mixed salad
fresh cilantro leaves

1 In a medium bowl, mix together the chicken pieces, ginger, garlic, chili powder, turmeric, salt, yogurt, lemon juice and fresh cilantro, and leave to marinate for at least 2 hours.

2 Place on a broiler tray or in a flameproof dish lined with foil and baste with the oil.

3 Preheat the broiler until medium hot. Broil the chicken for about 15–20 minutes until cooked, turning and basting 2–3 times. Serve with the garnish ingredients.

COOK'S TIP
This is a quick and easy Indian appetizer. It can also be served as a main course for four.

NUTRITION NOTES
Per portion:
Energy	131Kcals/552kJ
Fat	5.5g
Saturated fat	1.47g
Cholesterol	44.07mg

TUNA CHILI TACOS

...quick snack – ...to use both hands to eat them!

Makes 8

8 taco shells
14oz can red kidney beans, drained
½ cup low fat fromage frais
½ tsp chili sauce
2 scallions, chopped
1 tsp chopped fresh mint
½ small crisp lettuce, shredded
15oz can tuna chunks in water, drained
¾ cup shredded reduced-fat Cheddar cheese
8 cherry tomatoes, quartered
mint sprigs, to garnish

1 Warm the taco shells in a hot oven for a few minutes until crisp.

2 Mash the beans lightly with a fork, then stir in the fromage frais with the chili sauce, scallions, and mint.

3 Fill the taco shells with the shredded lettuce, the bean mixture, and tuna. Top the filled shells with the cheese and serve at once with the tomatoes, garnished with sprigs of mint.

NUTRITION NOTES

Per portion:

Energy	147Kcals/615kJ
Fat	2.42g
Saturated fat	1.13g
Cholesterol	29.69mg
Fiber	2.41g

POTATO SKINS WITH CAJUN DIP

No need to deep-fry potato skins for this treat – broiling crisps them up in no time.

Serves 2

2 large baking potatoes
½ cup plain yogurt
1 garlic clove, crushed
1 tsp tomato paste
½ tsp green chili paste (or ½ small green chili, chopped
¼ tsp celery salt
salt and black pepper

1 Bake or microwave the potatoes until tender. Cut them in half and scoop out the flesh, leaving a thin layer on the skins. Keep the scooped out potato for another meal.

2 Cut each potato in half again then place the pieces skin-side down on a large baking sheet.

3 Broil for 4–5 minutes, or until crisp. Mix together the dip ingredients and serve with the potato skins.

NUTRITION NOTES

Per portion:

Energy	202Kcals/847kJ
Fat	0.93g
Saturated fat	0.34g
Cholesterol	2.3mg
Fiber	3.03g

CHICKEN PITAS WITH RED COLESLAW

Pitas are convenient for simple snacks and lunch boxes and it's easy to load in lots of fresh healthy ingredients.

INGREDIENTS

Serves 4

¼ red cabbage, finely shredded
1 small red onion, finely sliced
2 radishes, thinly sliced
1 red apple, peeled, cored, and grated
1 tbsp lemon juice
3 tbsp low fat fromage frais
1 cooked chicken breast without skin,
    about 6oz
4 large pitas or 8 small pitas
salt and black pepper
chopped fresh parsley, to garnish

1 Remove the tough central spine from the cabbage leaves, then finely shred the leaves using a large sharp knife. Place the shredded cabbage in a bowl and stir in the onion, radishes, apple, and lemon juice.

2 Stir the fromage frais into the shredded cabbage mixture and season well with salt and pepper. Thinly slice the cooked chicken breast and stir into the shredded cabbage mixture until well coated in fromage frais.

3 Toast the pitas until warmed, then split them along one edge using a round-bladed knife. Spoon the filling into the pitas, then garnish with chopped fresh parsley.

COOK'S TIP
If the filled pitas need to be made more than an hour in advance, line the pita breads with crisp lettuce leaves before adding the filling.

NUTRITION NOTES

Per portion:

Energy	232Kcals/976kJ
Fat	2.61g
Saturated fat	0.76g
Cholesterol	24.61mg
Fiber	2.97g

WHOLE-WHEAT SLTs

A quick, tasty snack or easy packed lunch with a healthy combination – sardines, lettuce, and tomatoes!

INGREDIENTS

Serves 2

2 small whole-wheat rolls
4¼ oz can sardines in olive oil
4 crisp green lettuce leaves, such as
  Bibb
1 beefsteak tomato, sliced
juice of ½ lemon
salt and black pepper

1 Slice the rolls in half crosswise using a sharp knife. Drain off the oil from the sardines into a small bowl, then brush the cut surfaces of the rolls with a small amount of the oil.

2 Cut or break the sardines into small pieces, then fill each roll with a lettuce leaf, some sliced tomato, and pieces of sardine, sprinkling the filling with a little lemon juice, and salt and pepper to taste.

3 Sandwich the rolls back together and press the lids down lightly with your hand. Serve at once.

NUTRITION NOTES

Per portion:	
Energy	248Kcals/1042kJ
Fat	8.51g
Saturated fat	1.86g
Cholesterol	32.5mg
Fiber	3.01g

COOK'S TIP
As an alternative, replace the sardines with tuna packed in oil, or try mackerel fillets in oil and be generous with the black pepper.

SPINACH AND POTATO GALETTE

Creamy layers of potato, spinach and herbs make this a warming supper dish.

INGREDIENTS

Serves 6
2lb large potatoes
1lb fresh spinach
2 eggs
1¼ cups low fat cream cheese
1 tbsp grainy mustard
2 cups chopped mixed fresh herbs
 (such as chives, parsley, chervil
 or sorrel)
salt and black pepper
mixed salad, to serve

1 Preheat the oven to 350°F. Line a deep 9in cake pan with parchment paper. Place the potatoes in a large saucepan and cover with cold water. Bring to the boil and cook for about 10 minutes. Drain well and allow to cool slightly before slicing thinly.

2 Wash the spinach and place in a large pan with only the water that is clinging to the leaves. Cover and cook, stirring once, until the spinach has just wilted. Drain well in a strainer and squeeze out the excess moisture. Chop finely.

NUTRITION NOTES

Per portion:
Energy	255Kcals/1072kJ
Fat	9.13g
Saturated fat	4.28g
Cholesterol	81.82mg
Fiber	3.81g

3 Beat the eggs with the cream cheese and mustard, then stir in the chopped spinach and fresh herbs.

4 Place a layer of the sliced potatoes in the lined cake pan, arranging them in concentric circles. Top with a spoonful of the cream cheese mixture and spread out. Continue layering, seasoning with salt and pepper as you go, until all the potatoes and the cream cheese mixture are used up.

5 Cover the pan with a piece of foil and place in a roasting pan.

6 Fill the roasting pan with enough boiling water to come halfway up the sides, and cook in the oven for about 45–50 minutes. Serve hot or cold with a mixed salad.

SMOKED TROUT SALAD

Salads are the easy answer to fast, healthy eating. When lettuce is sweet and crisp, partner it with fillets of smoked trout, warm new potatoes and a creamy horseradish dressing.

INGREDIENTS

Serves 4
1½lb new potatoes
4 smoked trout fillets
4oz mixed lettuce leaves
4 slices dark rye bread, cut into fingers
salt and black pepper

For the dressing
4 tbsp horseradish cream
4 tbsp peanut oil
1 tbsp white wine vinegar
2 tsp caraway seeds

NUTRITION NOTES

Per portion:
Energy	487Kcals/2044kJ
Fat	22.22g
Saturated fat	4.1g
Cholesterol	52.1mg
Fiber	3.5g

2 Remove the skin from the trout, then pull out any little bones using your fingers or a pair of tweezers.

4 Flake the trout fillets and halve the potatoes. Scatter them together with the rye fingers over the salad leaves and toss to mix. Season to taste and serve.

1 Peel or scrub the potatoes. Place the potatoes in a large saucepan and cover with cold water. Bring to a boil and simmer for about 20 minutes.

3 To make the dressing, place all the ingredients in a screw-topped jar and shake vigorously. Season the lettuce leaves and moisten them with the prepared dressing. Divide the dressed leaves among four plates.

COOK'S TIP
To save time washing lettuce leaves, buy them ready-prepared from your supermarket. It is better to season the leaves rather than the dressing when making a salad.

SALMON PARCELS

Serve these little savory parcels just as they are for a snack, or with a pool of fresh tomato sauce for a special appetizer.

INGREDIENTS

Makes 12
3½oz can red or pink salmon
1 tbsp chopped fresh cilantro
4 scallions, finely chopped
4 sheets fila pastry
sunflower oil, for brushing
scallions and lettuce, to serve

COOK'S TIP
When you are using fila pastry, it is important to prevent it drying out; cover any you are not using with a dish towel or plastic wrap.

---

1 Preheat the oven to 400°F. Lightly oil a baking sheet. Drain the salmon, discarding any skin and bones, then place in a bowl.

2 Flake the salmon with a fork and mix with the fresh cilantro and scallions.

3 Place a single sheet of fila pastry on a work surface and brush lightly with oil. Place another sheet on top. Cut into six squares, each about 4in. Repeat with the remaining pastry, to make 12 squares.

4 Place a spoonful of the salmon mixture on each square. Brush the edges of the pastry with oil, then draw together, pressing to seal. Place on a baking sheet and bake for 12–15 minutes, until golden. Serve warm, with scallions and lettuce.

NUTRITION NOTES	
Per portion:	
Energy	25Kcals/107kJ
Fat	1.16g
Saturated fat	0.23g
Cholesterol	2.55mg
Fiber	0.05g

TOMATO-CHEESE TARTS

These crisp little tartlets are easier to make than they look. Best eaten fresh from the oven.

INGREDIENTS

Serves 4
2 sheets fila pastry
1 egg white
½ cup low fat cream cheese
handful fresh basil leaves
3 small tomatoes, sliced
salt and black pepper

1 Preheat the oven to 400°F. Brush the sheets of fila pastry lightly with egg white and cut into sixteen 4 in squares.

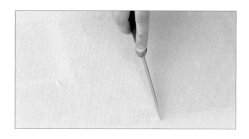

2 Layer the squares in twos, in eight muffin tins. Spoon the cheese into the pastry cases. Season with black pepper and top with basil leaves.

3 Arrange tomatoes on the tarts, add seasoning, and bake for 10-12 minutes, until golden. Serve warm.

NUTRITION NOTES	
Per portion:	
Energy	50Kcals/210kJ
Fat	0.33g
Saturated fat	0.05g
Cholesterol	0.29mg
Fiber	0.25g

MUSHROOM CROUSTADES

The rich mushroom flavor of this filling is heightened by the addition of Worcestershire sauce.

INGREDIENTS

Serves 2–4
1 short baguette, about 25cm/10in
2 tsp olive oil
9oz open cup mushrooms,
    quartered
2 tsp Worcestershire sauce
2 tsp lemon juice
2 tbsp skim milk
2 tbsp snipped fresh chives
salt and black pepper
snipped fresh chives, to garnish

1 Preheat the oven to 400°F. Cut the baguette in half lengthwise. Cut a scoop out of the soft middle of each using a sharp knife, leaving a thick border all the way around.

2 Brush the bread with oil, place on a baking sheet, and bake for about 6–8 minutes, until golden and crisp.

3 Place the mushrooms in a small saucepan with the Worcestershire sauce, lemon juice, and milk. Simmer for about 5 minutes, or until most of the liquid is evaporated.

4 Remove from the heat, then add the chives and seasoning. Spoon into the bread croustades and serve hot, garnished with snipped chives.

NUTRITION NOTES

Per portion:
Energy	324Kcals/1361kJ
Fat	6.4g
Saturated fat	1.27g
Cholesterol	0.3mg
Fiber	3.07g

TOMATO-PESTO TOASTIES

Ready-made pesto is high in fat but, as its flavor is so powerful, it can be used in very small amounts with good effect, as in these tasty toasties.

INGREDIENTS

Serves 2
2 thick slices crusty bread
3 tbsp low fat cream cheese or low fat fromage frais
2 tsp red or green pesto
1 beefsteak tomato
1 red onion
salt and black pepper

1 Place the bread slices under a hot broiler until golden brown on both sides, turning once. Leave to cool.

2 Mix together the low fat cream cheese and pesto in a small bowl until well blended, then spread thickly on the toasted bread.

3 Cut the beefsteak tomato and red onion, crosswise, into thin slices using a large sharp knife.

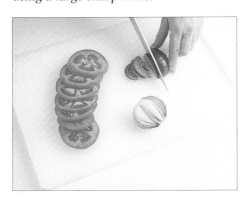

4 Arrange the slices, overlapping, on top of the toast and season with salt and pepper. Transfer the toasties to a broiler pan and broil until heated through, then serve immediately.

COOK'S TIP
Almost any type of crusty bread can be used for this recipe, but Italian olive oil bread and French bread will give the best flavor.

NUTRITION NOTES

Per portion:

Energy	177Kcals/741kJ
Fat	2.41g
Saturated fat	0.19g
Cholesterol	0.23mg
Fiber	2.2g

SMOKED SALMON CRÊPES WITH PESTO

These simple crêpes are quick to prepare and are perfect for a special occasion topped with smoked salmon, fresh basil and toasted pine nuts.

INGREDIENTS

Makes 12–16
½ cup skim milk
1 cup self-rising flour
1 egg
2 tbsp pesto sauce
vegetable oil, for frying
⅞ cup low fat sour cream
3oz smoked salmon
1 tbsp pine nuts, toasted
salt and black pepper
12–16 basil sprigs,
  to garnish

NUTRITION NOTES

Per portion:
Energy	116Kcals/485kJ
Fat	7.42g
Saturated fat	2.4g
Cholesterol	39.58mg
Fiber	0.34g

1 Pour half of the milk into a mixing bowl. Add the flour, egg, pesto sauce and seasoning, and mix to a smooth batter.

2 Add the remainder of the milk and stir until evenly blended.

3 Heat the vegetable oil in a large frying pan. Spoon the crêpe mixture into the heated oil in small heaps. Allow about 30 seconds for the crêpes to rise, then turn and cook briefly on the other side. Continue cooking the crêpes in batches until all the batter is used up.

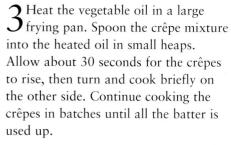

4 Arrange the crêpes on a serving plate and top each one with a spoonful of sour cream.

5 Cut the salmon into ½in strips and place on top of each crêpe.

6 Scatter each crêpe with pine nuts and garnish with a sprig of fresh basil before serving.

> COOK'S TIP
> If not serving immediately, cover the pancakes with a dish towel and keep warm in an oven preheated to 275°F.

WILD RICE RÖSTI WITH CARROT PURÉE

Rösti is a traditional dish from Switzerland. This variation has the extra nuttiness of wild rice and a bright simple sauce as a fresh accompaniment.

INGREDIENTS

Serves 6
½ cup wild rice
2lb large potatoes
3 tbsp walnut oil
1 tsp yellow mustard seeds
1 onion, coarsely grated and drained
2 tbsp fresh thyme leaves
salt and black pepper
vegetables, to serve

For the purée
12oz carrots, peeled and roughly chopped
pared rind and juice of 1 large orange

NUTRITION NOTES

Per portion:

Energy	246Kcals/1035kJ
Fat	8.72g
Saturated fat	0.78g
Cholesterol	0
Fiber	3.8g

1 For the purée, place the carrots in a saucepan, cover with cold water and add two pieces of orange rind. Bring to a boil and cook for about 10 minutes or until tender. Drain well and discard the rind.

2 Purée the mixture in a food processor or blender with 4 tbsp of the orange juice. Return to the pan.

3 Place the wild rice in a clean pan and cover with water. Bring to a boil and cook for 30–40 minutes, until the rice is just starting to split, but still crunchy. Drain the rice.

4 Scrub the potatoes, place in a large pan and cover with cold water. Bring to a boil and cook for about 10–15 minutes until just tender. Drain well and leave to cool slightly. When the potatoes are cool, peel and coarsely grate them into a large bowl. Add the cooked rice.

5 Heat 2 tbsp of the walnut oil in a nonstick frying pan and add the mustard seeds. When they start to pop, add the onion and cook gently for about 5 minutes until soft. Add to the bowl of potato and rice, together with the thyme, and mix thoroughly. Season.

6 Heat the remaining oil and add the potato mixture. Press down well and cook for about 10 minutes or until golden brown. Cover the pan with a plate and flip over, then slide the rösti back into the pan for 10 minutes more to cook the other side. Serve with the reheated carrot purée.

> COOK'S TIP
> Make individual rösti topped with a mixed julienne of vegetables for an unusual appetizer.

EGGPLANT SUNFLOWER PÂTÉ

INGREDIENTS

Serves 4
1 large eggplant
1 garlic clove, crushed
1 tbsp lemon juice
2 tbsp sunflower seeds
3 tbsp plain low fat yogurt
handful fresh cilantro or parsley
black pepper
black olives, to garnish

1 Cut the eggplant in half and place, cut-side down, on a baking sheet. Place under a hot broiler for 15–20 minutes, until the skin is blackened and the flesh is soft. Leave for a few minutes, to cool slightly.

2 Scoop the flesh of the eggplant into a food processor. Add the garlic, lemon juice, sunflower seeds, and yogurt. Process until smooth.

3 Coarsely chop the fresh cilantro or parsley and mix in. Season, then spoon into a serving dish. Top with olives and serve with vegetable sticks.

NUTRITION NOTES	
Per portion:	
Energy	71Kcals/298kJ
Fat	4.51g
Saturated fat	0.48g
Cholesterol	0.45mg
Fiber	2.62g

BELL PEPPER DIPS WITH CRUDITÉS

Make one or both of these colorful vegetable dips – if you have time to make both they look spectacular together.

INGREDIENTS

Serves 4–6
2 medium red bell peppers, halved and seeded
2 medium yellow bell peppers, halved and seeded
2 garlic cloves
2 tbsp lemon juice
4 tsp olive oil
½ cup fresh white bread crumbs
salt and black pepper
fresh vegetables, for dipping

1 Place the bell peppers in separate saucepans with a peeled clove of garlic. Add just enough water to cover.

2 Bring to a boil, then cover and simmer for 15 minutes until tender. Drain, cool, then purée separately in a food processor or blender, adding half the lemon juice and olive oil to each.

3 Stir half the bread crumbs into each and season to taste with salt and pepper. Serve the dips with a selection of fresh vegetables for dipping.

NUTRITION NOTES	
Per portion:	
Energy	103Kcals/432kJ
Fat	3.7g
Saturated fat	0.47g
Cholesterol	0
Fiber	2.77g

MEAT DISHES

There's no reason why meat should not be a valuable part of a low fat, low cholesterol diet, but you need to make careful choices when shopping, and adapt preparation and cooking methods to keep fats to a minimum. Remember that even lean meat has hidden fat, so broiling or roasting on a rack is an advantage, and any added fats should be low in saturates and used in moderation. A fat-trimmed roast needn't be dry, especially if you seal it with a moist, savory crust as in Pork Roast in a Blanket. Even for casseroles, there's often no need to seal the meat in fat first – a nonstick pan will seal the meat in its own fat. Or choose stir-frying, which quickly seals the meat with just a touch of oil.

PORK AND CELERY POPOVERS

Lower in fat than they look, and a good way to make the meat go further, these little popovers will be popular with children.

INGREDIENTS

Serves 4
sunflower oil, for brushing
1¼ cup flour
1 egg white
1 cup skim milk
½ cup water
12 oz lean ground pork
2 celery stalks, finely chopped
3 tbsp oatmeal
2 tbsp snipped chives
1 tbsp Worcestershire sauce
salt and black pepper

1 Preheat the oven to 425°F. Brush 12 deep muffin pans with a small amount of oil.

2 Place the flour in a bowl and make a well in the center. Add the egg white and milk and gradually beat in the flour. Gradually add the water, beating until smooth and bubbly.

3 Place the ground pork, celery, oatmeal, chives, Worcestershire sauce, and seasoning in a bowl and mix well. Mold the mixture into 12 small balls and place in the muffin pans.

4 Cook for 10 minutes, remove from the oven, and quickly pour the batter into the pans. Cook for 20–25 minutes more, or until puffed and golden brown. Serve hot with thin gravy and fresh vegetables.

NUTRITION NOTES	
Per portion:	
Energy	344Kcals/1443kJ
Fat	9.09g
Saturated fat	2.7g
Cholesterol	61.62mg
Fiber	2.37g

BEEF AND MUSHROOM BURGERS

It's worth making your own burgers to cut down on fat – in these the meat is extended with mushrooms for extra fiber.

INGREDIENTS

Serves 4

1 small onion, chopped
2 cups small cup mushrooms
1 lb lean ground beef
1 cup fresh whole-wheat bread crumbs
1 tsp dried mixed herbs
1 tbsp tomato paste
flour, for shaping
salt and black pepper

1 Place the onion and mushrooms in a food processor and process until finely chopped. Add the beef, bread crumbs, herbs, tomato paste and seasonings. Process for a few seconds, until the mixture binds together but still has some texture.

2 Divide the mixture into 8–10 pieces, then press into burger shapes using lightly floured hands.

3 Cook the burgers in a nonstick skillet, or under a hot broiler for 12-15 minutes, turning once, until evenly cooked. Serve with relish and lettuce, in burger buns or pita bread.

COOK'S TIP
The mixture is soft, so handle carefully and use a metal spatula for turning to prevent the burgers from breaking during cooking.

NUTRITION NOTES

Per portion:	
Energy	196Kcals/822kJ
Fat	5.9g
Saturated fat	2.21g
Cholesterol	66.37mg
Fiber	1.6g

CURRIED LAMB AND LENTILS

This colorful curry is packed with protein and low in fat.

INGREDIENTS

Serves 4
8 lean, boneless lamb leg steaks, about 1¼ lb total weight
1 medium onion, chopped
2 medium carrots, diced
1 celery stalk, chopped
1 tbsp hot curry paste
2 tbsp tomato paste
2 cups broth
1 cup green lentils
salt and black pepper
fresh cilantro leaves, to garnish
boiled rice, to serve

1 In a large, nonstick pan, cook the lamb steaks without fat until browned, turning once.

2 Add the vegetables and cook for 2 minutes, then stir in the curry paste, tomato paste, broth, and lentils.

3 Bring to a boil, cover, and simmer gently for 30 minutes until tender. Add more broth, if necessary. Season and serve with cilantro and rice.

NUTRITION NOTES	
Per portion:	
Energy	375Kcals/1575kJ
Fat	13.03g
Saturated fat	5.34g
Cholesterol	98.75mg
Fiber	6.11g

GOLDEN PORK AND APRICOT CASSEROLE

The rich golden color and warm spicy flavor of this simple casserole make it ideal for chilly winter days.

INGREDIENTS

Serves 4
4 lean pork loin chops
1 medium onion, thinly sliced
2 yellow bell peppers, seeded and sliced
2 tsp medium hot curry powder
1 tbsp flour
1 cup chicken broth
⅔ cup dried apricots
2 tbsp whole-grain mustard
salt and black pepper

1 Trim the excess fat from the pork and cook without fat in a large, heavy or nonstick pan until lightly browned.

2 Add the onion and bell peppers to the pan and stir over moderate heat for 5 minutes. Stir in the curry powder and the flour.

3 Add the broth, stirring, then add the apricots and mustard. Cover and simmer for 25–30 minutes, until tender. Adjust the seasoning and serve hot, with rice or new potatoes.

NUTRITION NOTES	
Per portion:	
Energy	289Kcals/1213kJ
Fat	10.03g
Saturated fat	3.23g
Cholesterol	82.8mg
Fiber	4.86g

COUNTRY PORK WITH PARSLEY COBBLER

This hearty casserole is a complete main course in one pot.

INGREDIENTS

Serves 4
1 lb boneless pork shoulder, diced
1 small rutabaga, diced
2 carrots, sliced
2 parsnips, sliced
2 leeks, sliced
2 celery stalks, sliced
3⅔ cups boiling beef broth
2 tbsp tomato paste
2 tbsp chopped fresh parsley
¼ cup pearl barley
celery salt and black pepper

For the topping
1 cup flour
1 tsp baking powder
6 tbsp low fat fromage frais
3 tbsp chopped fresh parsley

1 Preheat the oven to 350°. Cook the pork without fat, in a nonstick pan until lightly browned.

2 Add the vegetables to the pan and stir over medium heat until lightly colored. Tip into a large casserole dish, then stir in the broth, tomato paste, parsley, and pearl barley.

3 Season with celery salt and pepper, then cover and place in the oven for about 1–1¼ hours, until the pork and vegetables are tender.

4 For the topping, sift the flour and baking powder with seasoning, then stir in the fromage frais and parsley with enough cold water to mix to a soft dough. Roll out to about ½ inch thickness and cut into 12–16 triangles.

5 Remove the casserole from the oven and raise the temperature to 425°F.

6 Arrange the triangles over the casserole, overlapping. Bake for 15–20 minutes, until puffed and golden.

NUTRITION NOTES

Per portion:
Energy	461Kcals/1936kJ
Fat	10.55g
Saturated fat	3.02g
Cholesterol	77.85mg
Fiber	9.44g

BEEF STRIPS WITH ORANGE AND GINGER

Stir-frying is one of the best ways to cook with the minimum of fat. It's also one of the quickest ways to cook, but you do need to choose tender meat.

— INGREDIENTS —

Serves 4

*1 lb lean beef rump, fillet, or sirloin,
    cut into thin strips*
finely grated rind and juice of 1 orange
1 tbsp light soy sauce
1 tsp cornstarch
*1in piece ginger root, finely
    chopped*
2 tsp sesame oil
1 large carrot, cut into thin strips
2 scallions, thinly sliced

1 Place the beef strips in a bowl and sprinkle over the orange rind and juice. If possible, leave to marinate for at least 30 minutes.

2 Drain the liquid from the meat and set aside, then mix the meat with the soy sauce, cornstarch, and ginger.

3 Heat the oil in a wok or large frying pan and add the beef. Stir-fry for 1 minute until lightly colored, then add the carrot and stir-fry for 2–3 minutes more.

4 Stir in the scallions and reserved liquid, then cook, stirring, until boiling and thickened. Serve **hot with** rice noodles or plain boiled rice.

— NUTRITION NOTES —

Per portion:	
Energy	175Kcals/730kJ
Fat	6.81g
Saturated fat	2.31g
Cholesterol	66.37mg
Fiber	0.67g

GREEK LAMB PIE

INGREDIENTS

Serves 4

sunflower oil, for brushing
1 lb lean ground lamb
1 medium onion, sliced
1 garlic clove, crushed
14oz can plum tomatoes
2 tbsp chopped fresh mint
1 tsp ground nutmeg
12oz young spinach leaves
10 oz packet fila pastry
1 tsp sesame seeds
salt and black pepper

1 Preheat the oven to 400°F. Lightly oil a 8½ in round spring form pan.

2 Cook the lamb and onion without fat in a nonstick pan until golden. Add the garlic, tomatoes, mint, nutmeg, and seasoning. Bring to a boil, stirring. Simmer, stirring occasionally, until most of the liquid has evaporated.

3 Wash the spinach and remove any tough stalks, then cook in only the water clinging to the leaves for about 2 minutes, until wilted.

4 Lightly brush each sheet of fila pastry with oil and lay in overlapping layers in the pan, leaving enough overhanging to wrap over the top.

5 Spoon in the meat and spinach, then wrap the pastry over to enclose, scrunching it slightly. Sprinkle with sesame seeds and bake for about 25–30 minutes, or until golden and crisp. Serve hot, with salad or vegetables.

NUTRITION NOTES

Per portion:

Energy	444Kcals/1865kJ
Fat	15.36g
Saturated fat	5.51g
Cholesterol	88.87mg
Fiber	3g

PORK ROAST IN A BLANKET

INGREDIENTS

Serves 4

3 lb lean pork loin joint
1 eating apple, cored and grated
¾ cup fresh bread crumbs
2 tbsp chopped hazelnuts
1 tbsp Dijon mustard
1 tbsp snipped fresh chives
salt and black pepper

1 If necessary, trim the roast, leaving only a thin layer of fat.

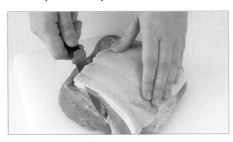

2 Preheat the oven to 425°F. Place the meat on a rack in a roasting pan, cover the meat with foil, and roast for 1 hour, then reduce the oven temperature to 350°F.

3 Mix together the apple, bread crumbs, nuts, mustard, chives, and seasoning. Remove the foil and spread the bread crumb mixture over the fat surface of the meat.

4 Roast the pork for 45–60 minutes, or until the juices run clear. Serve in slices with gravy.

NUTRITION NOTES

Per portion:

Energy	367Kcals/1540kJ
Fat	18.73g
Saturated fat	5.19g
Cholesterol	129.38mg
Fiber	1.5g

STUFFED EGGPLANT WITH LAMB

Serves 4

2 eggplants
2 tbsp sunflower oil
1 onion, sliced
1in piece fresh ginger root, chopped
1 tsp chili powder
1 garlic clove, crushed
¼ tsp turmeric
1 tsp salt
1 tsp ground cilantro
1 tomato, chopped
12oz lean ground lamb
1 green bell pepper, roughly chopped
1 orange bell pepper, roughly chopped
2 tbsp chopped fresh cilantro

For the garnish

½ onion, sliced
2 cherry tomatoes, quartered
fresh cilantro leaves

NUTRITION NOTES

Per portion:
Energy	239Kcals/1003kJ
Fat	13.92g
Saturated fat	4.36g
Cholesterol	67.15mg

1 Cut the eggplants in half lengthwise and cut out most of the flesh and discard. Place the eggplant shells in a lightly greased ovenproof dish.

2 In a saucepan, heat 1 tbsp oil and fry the onion until golden. Gradually stir in the ginger, chili powder, garlic, turmeric, salt and ground cilantro. Add the tomato, lower the heat and stir-fry for 5 minutes.

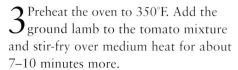

3 Preheat the oven to 350°F. Add the ground lamb to the tomato mixture and stir-fry over medium heat for about 7–10 minutes more.

4 Add the chopped bell peppers and fresh cilantro to the lamb mixture, and stir well.

5 Spoon the lamb mixture into the eggplant shells and brush the edges of the shells with the remaining oil. Bake in the preheated oven for about 20–25 minutes until cooked through and browned on top.

6 Serve with the garnish ingredients and either a green salad or plain boiled rice.

COOK'S TIP
For a special occasion, stuffed baby eggplants look particularly attractive. Use four small eggplants, leaving the stalks intact, and prepare and cook as described above. Reduce the baking time slightly, if necessary. Large tomatoes or zucchini also make a good alternative to using eggplants for the recipe.

BEEF WITH GREEN BEANS

This easy-to-cook curried dish is a delicious variation on a traditional Indian recipe.

INGREDIENTS

Serves 4

10oz fine green beans, cut into 1in pieces
2 tbsp sunflower oil
1 onion, sliced
1in piece fresh ginger root, chopped
1 garlic clove, crushed
1 tsp chili powder
1¼ tsp salt
¼ tsp turmeric
2 tomatoes, chopped
1lb lean beef, cubed
5 cups water
1 tbsp chopped fresh cilantro
1 red bell pepper, sliced
2 green chilies, chopped

1 Cook the green beans in a saucepan of boiling salted water for about 5 minutes, then drain and set aside.

2 Heat the oil in a large saucepan and fry the sliced onion until golden.

3 Mix together the ginger, garlic, chili powder, salt, turmeric and chopped tomatoes. Spoon into the onions and stir-fry for about 5–7 minutes.

4 Add the beef and stir-fry for about 3 minutes more. Pour in the water, bring to a boil and lower the heat. Cover and cook for about 45–60 minutes until most of the water has evaporated and the meat is tender.

5 Add the green beans to the pan and mix everything together well.

6 Finally, add the red bell pepper, fresh cilantro and chopped green chilies and cook for 7–10 minutes more stirring occasionally. Serve hot with whole-wheat chapatis.

NUTRITION NOTES

Per portion:

Energy	241Kcals/1012kJ
Fat	11.6g
Saturated fat	2.89g
Cholesterol	66.96mg

MEXICAN BEEF BURGERS

Nothing beats the flavor and quality of a homemade burger. This version is from Mexico and is delicately seasoned with cumin and fresh cilantro.

INGREDIENTS

Makes 4

4 corn cobs
1 cup stale white breadcrumbs
6 tbsp skim milk
1 small onion, finely chopped
1 tsp ground cumin
½ tsp cayenne pepper
½ tsp celery salt
3 tbsp chopped fresh cilantro
2lb lean ground beef
4 sesame buns
4 tbsp reduced calorie mayonnaise
4 tomato slices
½ iceberg lettuce or other leaves such as frisée or Romaine
salt and black pepper
1 large packet corn chips, to serve

1 Cook the corn cobs in a large saucepan of boiling water for about 15 minutes.

2 Place the breadcrumbs, milk, onion, cumin, cayenne, celery salt and fresh cilantro in a large bowl and mix together thoroughly.

3 Add the beef and mix by hand until the mixture is evenly blended.

4 Divide the beef mixture into four and flatten in sheets of plastic wrap.

5 Preheat a moderate broiler and cook for about 10 minutes for medium burgers or 15 minutes for well-done burgers.

6 Split and toast the buns, spread with mayonnaise and sandwich the burgers with tomato, lettuce and seasoning. Serve with corn chips and the corn cobs.

NUTRITION NOTES	
Per portion:	
Energy	563Kcals/2363kJ
Fat	18.82g
Saturated fat	5.55g
Cholesterol	133.2mg

PORK STEAKS WITH GREMOLATA

Gremolata is a popular Italian dressing of garlic, lemon and parsley – it adds a hint of sharpness to the pork.

INGREDIENTS

Serves 4
2 tbsp olive oil
4 lean pork shoulder steaks, about
  6oz each
1 onion, chopped
2 garlic cloves, crushed
2 tbsp tomato paste
14oz can chopped tomatoes
⅔ cup dry white wine
bouquet garni
3 anchovy fillets, drained and chopped
salt and black pepper
salad leaves, to serve

For the gremolata
3 tbsp chopped fresh parsley
grated rind of ½ lemon
grated rind of 1 lime
1 garlic clove, chopped

1 Heat the oil in a large flameproof casserole, add the pork steaks and brown on both sides. Remove the steaks from the casserole.

2 Add the onion to the casserole and cook until soft and beginning to brown. Add the garlic and cook for about 1–2 minutes, then stir in the tomato paste, chopped tomatoes and wine. Add the bouquet garni. Bring to a boil, then boil rapidly for 3–4 minutes to reduce the sauce and thicken slightly.

3 Return the pork to the casserole, then cover and cook for about 30 minutes. Stir in the anchovies.

4 Cover the casserole and cook for 15 minutes more, or until the pork is tender. To make the gremolata, mix together the parsley, lemon and lime rinds and garlic.

5 Remove the pork steaks and discard the bouquet garni. Reduce the sauce over a high heat, if it is not already thick. Taste and adjust the seasoning if you wish.

6 Return the pork to the casserole, then sprinkle with the gremolata. Cover and cook for 5 minutes more, then serve hot with salad leaves.

NUTRITION NOTES	
Per portion:	
Energy	267Kcals/1121kJ
Fat	13.39g
Saturated fat	3.43g
Cholesterol	69mg
Fiber	2.06g

PAN-FRIED MEDITERRANEAN LAMB

The warm summery flavors of the Mediterranean are combined for a simple weekday meal.

INGREDIENTS

Serves 4
8 lean lamb rib chops
1 medium onion, thinly sliced
2 red bell peppers, seeded and sliced
14oz can plum tomatoes
1 garlic clove, crushed
3 tbsp chopped fresh basil leaves
2 tbsp chopped black olives
salt and black pepper

1 Trim any excess fat from the lamb, then cook without fat in a nonstick pan until golden brown.

2 Add the onion and bell peppers to the pan. Cook, stirring, for a few minutes to soften, then add the plum tomatoes, garlic, and basil.

3 Cover and simmer for 20 minutes or until the lamb is tender. Stir in the olives, season, and serve hot with pasta.

NUTRITION NOTES

Per portion:

Energy	224Kcals/939kJ
Fat	10.17g
Saturated fat	4.32g
Cholesterol	79mg
Fiber	2.48g

BACON KOFTAS

These easy koftas are good for outdoor summer barbecues, served with lots of salad.

INGREDIENTS

Serves 4
8oz lean bacon, coarsely chopped
1 cup fresh whole-wheat bread crumbs
2 scallions, chopped
15ml/1 tbsp chopped fresh parsley
finely grated rind of 1 lemon
1 egg white
black pepper
paprika
lemon rind and fresh parsley leaves, to garnish

1 Place the bacon in a food processor together with the bread crumbs, scallions, parsley, lemon rind, egg white, and pepper. Process the mixture until it is finely chopped and begins to bind together.

2 Divide the bacon mixture into eight, even-sized pieces and shape into long ovals around eight wooden or bamboo skewers.

3 Sprinkle the koftas with paprika and cook under a hot broiler or on a barbecue for about 8–10 minutes, turning occasionally, until browned and cooked through. Garnish with lemon rind and parsley leaves, then serve hot with lemon rice and salad.

NUTRITION NOTES

Per portion:

Energy	128Kcals/538kJ
Fat	4.7g
Saturated fat	1.61g
Cholesterol	10.13mg
Fiber	1.33g

SAUSAGE AND BEANS WITH DUMPLINGS

Sausages needn't be totally banned on a low fat diet, but choose them carefully. If you are unable to find a reduced-fat variety, choose turkey sausages instead, and always drain off any fat during cooking.

INGREDIENTS

Serves 4
1 lb half-fat sausages
1 medium onion, thinly sliced
1 green bell pepper, seeded and diced
1 small red chili, sliced, or ½ tsp chili sauce
14oz can chopped tomatoes
1 cup beef broth
15oz can red kidney beans, drained
salt and black pepper

For the dumplings
2½ cups flour
2 tsp baking powder
1 cup cottage cheese

1 Cook the sausages without fat in a nonstick pan until brown. Add the onion and pepper. Stir in the chili, tomatoes, and broth; bring to a boil.

NUTRITION NOTES

Per portion:
Energy	574Kcals/2409kJ
Fat	13.09g
Saturated fat	0.15g
Cholesterol	52.31mg
Fiber	9.59g

2 Cover and simmer gently for 15–20 minutes, then add the beans and bring to a boil.

3 To make the dumplings, sift the flour and baking powder together and add enough water to mix to a firm dough. Roll out thinly and stamp out 16–18 rounds using a 3in cutter.

4 Place a small spoonful of cottage cheese on each round and bring the edges of the dough together, pinching to enclose. Arrange the dumplings over the sausages in the pan, cover the pan, and simmer for 10–12 minutes, until the dumplings are puffed. Serve hot.

SPICY SPRING LAMB ROAST

INGREDIENTS

Serves 6

3–3½lb lean leg spring lamb
1 tsp chili powder
1 garlic clove, crushed
1 tsp ground cilantro
1 tsp ground cumin
1 tsp salt
2 tsp shredded coconut
2 tsp ground almonds
3 tbsp plain low fat yogurt
2 tbsp lemon juice
2 tbsp golden raisins
2 tbsp corn oil

For the garnish

mixed salad leaves
fresh cilantro leaves
2 tomatoes, sliced
1 large carrot, cut into julienne strips
lemon wedges

NUTRITION NOTES

Per portion:

Energy	197Kcals/825kJ
Fat	11.96g
Saturated fat	4.7g
Cholesterol	67.38mg

1 Preheat the oven to 350°F. Trim off the fat, rinse and pat dry the leg of lamb and set aside on a sheet of foil large enough to enclose the whole joint.

2 In a medium bowl, mix together the chili powder, garlic, ground cilantro, ground cumin and salt.

3 In a food processor or blender, process together the shredded coconut, ground almonds, yogurt, lemon juice and golden raisins until you have a smooth texture.

4 Add the contents of the food processor to the spice mixture together with the corn oil and mix together. Pour this on to the leg of lamb and rub over the meat.

5 Enclose the meat in the foil and place in an ovenproof dish. Cook in the preheated oven for 1½ hours.

6 Remove the lamb from the oven, open the foil and, using the back of a spoon, spread the mixture evenly over the meat again. Return the lamb, uncovered, to the oven for 45 minutes more or until it is cooked right through and tender. Slice the meat and serve with the garnish ingredients.

Lamb Pie with Potato Crust

A pleasant change from meat and potatoes – healthier, too.

Ingredients

Serves 4

1½ lb potatoes, diced
2 tbsp skim milk
1 tbsp whole-grain or French mustard
1 lb lean ground lamb
1 onion, chopped
2 celery stalks, sliced
2 carrots, diced
⅔ cup beef broth
4 tbsp oatmeal
1 tbsp Worcestershire sauce
2 tbsp fresh chopped rosemary, or
  2 tsp dried
salt and black pepper

1 Cook the potatoes in boiling, lightly salted water until tender. Drain and mash until smooth, then stir in the milk and mustard. Meanwhile, preheat the oven to 400°F.

2 Break up the lamb with a fork and cook without fat in a nonstick pan until lightly browned. Add the onion, celery, and carrots to the pan and cook for 2–3 minutes, stirring.

3 Stir in the broth and oatmeal. Bring to a boil, then add the Worcestershire sauce and rosemary, and season to taste with salt and pepper.

4 Turn the meat mixture into a 1.8 litre/3 pint/7 cup ovenproof dish and spread over the potato topping evenly, swirling with the edge of a knife. Bake for 30–35 minutes, or until golden. Serve hot with fresh vegetables.

Nutrition Notes

Per portion:

Energy	422Kcals/1770kJ
Fat	12.41g
Saturated fat	5.04g
Cholesterol	89.03mg
Fiber	5.07g

INDONESIAN PORK AND PEANUT SATÉ

These delicious skewers of pork are popular street food in Indonesia. They are quick to make and eat.

INGREDIENTS

Serves 4

2 cups long grain rice
1lb lean pork
pinch of salt
2 limes, quartered, and a chili,
* to garnish*
green salad, to serve

For the sauce

1 tbsp sunflower oil
1 small onion, chopped
1 garlic clove, crushed
½ tsp hot chili sauce
1 tbsp sugar
2 tbsp soy sauce
2 tbsp lemon or lime juice
½ tsp anchovy paste (optional)
4 tbsp smooth peanut butter

1 Place the rice in a large saucepan, and cover with 3¾ cups of boiling salted water, stir and bring to a boil. Reduce the heat and simmer uncovered for about 15 minutes until the liquid has been absorbed. Switch off the heat, cover and stand for 5 minutes.

2 Slice the pork into thin strips, then thread zig-zag fashion on to sixteen bamboo skewers.

3 To make the sauce, very gently heat the sunflower oil in a pan. Add the onion and cook over a low heat to soften without coloring for about 3–4 minutes. Add the next five ingredients and the anchovy paste, if using. Simmer briefly, then gently stir in the smooth peanut butter.

COOK'S TIP
Indonesian saté can be prepared with lean beef, chicken or shrimp for a delicious alternative.

4 Arrange the skewers on a baking tray and spoon over a third of the sauce. Broil for 6–8 minutes, turning once. Serve on a bed of rice, accompanied by the remaining sauce. Garnish with the limes and chili and serve with a salad.

NUTRITION NOTES

Per portion:

Energy	689Kcals/2895kJ
Fat	21.07g
Saturated fat	4.95g
Cholesterol	77.62mg
Fiber	1.39g

RUBY PORK CHOPS

This sweet, tangy sauce works well with lean pork chops.

INGREDIENTS

Serves 4
1 ruby grapefruit
4 lean boneless pork chops
3 tbsp red currant jelly
black pepper

NUTRITION NOTES

Per portion:
Energy	215Kcals/904kJ
Fat	8.40g
Saturated fat	3.02g
Cholesterol	20.25mg
Fiber	0.81g

1 Cut away all the peel and pith from the grapefruit, using a sharp knife, and carefully remove the segments, catching the juice in a bowl.

2 Cook the pork chops in a nonstick skillet without fat, turning them once, until golden and cooked.

3 Add the reserved grapefruit juice and red currant jelly to the pan and stir until melted. Add the grapefruit segments, then season with pepper, and serve hot with fresh vegetables.

JAMAICAN BEAN STEW

If pumpkin is not available, use any other type of squash, or try rutabaga instead. This recipe is a good one to double – or even triple – for a crowd.

INGREDIENTS

Serves 4
1 lb stewing beef, diced
1 small pumpkin, about 1 lb, flesh diced
1 medium onion, chopped
1 green bell pepper, seeded and sliced
1 tbsp paprika
2 garlic cloves, crushed
1 in piece fresh ginger root, chopped
14oz can chopped tomatoes
1 cup baby corn
1 cup beef broth
15oz can chick-peas, drained
15oz can red kidney beans, drained
salt and black pepper

1 Cook the diced beef without fat in a large flameproof casserole, stirring to seal it on all sides.

2 Stir in the pumpkin, onion, and pepper, cook for 2 minutes more, then add the paprika, garlic, and ginger.

3 Stir in the tomatoes, corn, and broth, then bring to a boil. Cover and simmer for 40–45 minutes or until tender. Add the chick peas and beans, and heat thoroughly. Adjust the seasoning with salt and pepper to taste. Serve hot, with couscous or rice.

NUTRITION NOTES

Per portion:
Energy	357Kcals/1500kJ
Fat	8.77g
Saturated fat	2.11g
Cholesterol	66.37mg
Fiber	10.63g

BUTTERFLIED CUMIN AND GARLIC LAMB

Ground cumin and garlic give the lamb a wonderful Middle-Eastern flavor, although you may prefer a simple oil, lemon and herb marinade instead.

INGREDIENTS

Serves 6
4–4½lb lean leg of lamb
4 tbsp olive oil
2 tbsp ground cumin
4–6 garlic cloves, crushed
salt and black pepper
cilantro leaves and lemon wedges,
   to garnish
toasted almond and raisin-studded rice,
   to serve

1 To butterfly the lamb, cut away the meat from the bone using a small sharp knife. Remove any excess fat and the thin, parchment-like membrane. Bat out the meat to an even thickness, then prick the fleshy side of the lamb well with the tip of a knife.

2 In a bowl, mix together the oil, cumin and garlic, and season with pepper. Spoon the mixture all over the lamb, then rub it well into the crevices. Cover and leave to marinate overnight.

3 Preheat the oven to 400°F. Spread the lamb, skin-side down, on a rack in a roasting pan. Season with salt, and roast for about 45–60 minutes, until crusty brown outside, but still pink in the center.

4 Remove the lamb from the oven and leave it to rest for about 10 minutes. Cut into diagonal slices and serve with the toasted almond and raisin-studded rice. Garnish with cilantro leaves and lemon wedges.

NUTRITION NOTES

Per portion:
Energy	387Kcals/1624kJ
Fat	24.42g
Saturated fat	8.72g
Cholesterol	144.83mg
Fiber	0.14g

COOK'S TIP
The lamb may be barbecued – thread it on to two long skewers and cook on a hot barbecue for 20–25 minutes on each side.

SKEWERS OF LAMB WITH MINT

A delicious way to serve lamb with a Mediterranean twist. This dish could also be cooked on a barbecue and eaten al fresco-style in the garden.

INGREDIENTS

Serves 4

1¼ cups plain low fat yogurt
½ garlic clove, crushed
good pinch of saffron powder
2 tbsp chopped fresh mint
2 tbsp clear honey
3 tbsp olive oil
3 lean lamb neck fillets, about 1½lb
  in total
1 eggplant
2 small red onions, quartered
salt and black pepper
small mint leaves,
  to garnish
lettuce and hot pita bread,
  to serve

COOK'S TIP
If using bamboo skewers, soak them in cold water before use to prevent them burning. All lean, not too thick, cuts of meat such as lamb or chicken cook very well on a barbecue. Meat should be marinated beforehand and left overnight if at all possible.

2 Trim the lamb and cut into 1in cubes. Add to the marinade and stir until well coated. Leave to marinate for at least 4 hours.

4 Preheat the broiler. Remove the lamb cubes from the marinade. Thread the lamb, eggplant and onion pieces alternately on to skewers. Broil for about 10–12 minutes, turning and basting occasionally with the marinade, until the lamb is tender. Serve the skewers on a bed of lettuce, garnished with mint leaves and accompanied by hot pita bread.

1 In a shallow dish, mix together the yogurt, garlic, saffron, mint, honey, oil and ground black pepper.

3 Cut the eggplant into 1in cubes and blanch in boiling salted water for 1–2 minutes. Drain well.

NUTRITION NOTES	
Per portion:	
Energy	484Kcals/2032kJ
Fat	30.35g
Saturated fat	12.54g
Cholesterol	143.06mg
Fiber	2.05g

PAN-FRIED PORK WITH PEACHES

INGREDIENTS

Serves 4

2 cups long grain rice
4 cups chicken broth
4 lean pork chops or loin pieces, about
  7oz each
2 tbsp vegetable oil
2 tbsp dark rum or sherry
1 small onion, chopped
3 large ripe peaches
1 tbsp green peppercorns
1 tbsp white wine vinegar
salt and black pepper
flat leaf parsley, to garnish

NUTRITION NOTES

Per portion:
Energy	679Kcals/2852kJ
Fat	16.09g
Saturated fat	3.98g
Cholesterol	89.7mg
Fiber	1.84g

1 Place the rice in a large saucepan and cover with 3¾ cups chicken broth. Stir, bring to a boil, then reduce the heat and simmer uncovered for about 15 minutes. Switch off the heat, cover, and leave for 5 minutes. Season the pork. Heat a large metal frying pan and moisten the pork with 1 tbsp of the oil. Cook for about 12 minutes, turning once.

2 Transfer the meat to a warm plate. Pour off the excess fat from the pan and return to the heat. Allow the sediment to sizzle and brown, add the rum or sherry and loosen the sediment with a flat wooden spoon. Pour the pan contents over the meat, cover and keep warm. Wipe the pan clean.

3 Heat the remaining vegetable oil in the pan and soften the onion over a gentle heat.

4 Cover the peaches with boiling water to loosen the skins, then peel, slice and discard the pits.

5 Add the peaches and peppercorns to the onion and cook for about 3–4 minutes, until they begin to soften.

6 Add the remaining chicken broth and simmer briefly. Return the pork and meat juices to the pan, sharpen with vinegar, and season to taste. Serve the pork and peaches with the rice and garnish with flat leaf parsley.

COOK'S TIP
Unripe peaches are unsuitable for this recipe. A can of sliced peaches may be used instead.

TURKISH LAMB AND APRICOT STEW

The chick-peas and almonds give a delightful crunchiness to this wholesome stew.

INGREDIENTS

Serves 4

1 large eggplant, cubed
2 tbsp sunflower oil
1 onion, chopped
1 garlic clove, crushed
1 tsp ground cinnamon
3 whole cloves
1 lb lean boneless leg of lamb, cubed
14oz can chopped tomatoes
⅔ cup ready-to-eat dried apricots
4oz canned chick-peas, drained
1 tsp clear honey
salt and black pepper
chopped fresh parsley, and 2 tbsp chopped almonds, fried in a little oil, to garnish
couscous, to serve

1 Place the eggplant in a colander, sprinkle with salt and leave for 30 minutes. Heat the oil in a flameproof casserole, add the onion and garlic and fry for about 5 minutes.

NUTRITION NOTES

Per portion:

Energy	360 kcals/1512 kJ
Fat	17.05 g
Saturated fat	5.46g
Cholesterol	88.87mg
Fiber	6.16g

2 Stir in the ground cinnamon and cloves and fry for about 1 minute. Add the lamb and cook for 5–6 minutes more, stirring occasionally until it is well browned.

3 Rinse, drain and pat dry the eggplant, add to the pan and cook for about 3 minutes, stirring well. Add the tomatoes, 1¼ cups water, the apricots and seasoning. Bring to a boil, then cover the pan and simmer gently for about 45 minutes.

4 Stir in the chick-peas and honey, and cook for 15–20 minutes more, or until the lamb is tender. Serve the stew accompanied by couscous mixed with a little chopped parsley and garnished with the almonds.

COOK'S TIP
Grains are full of proteins and vitamins, and chick-peas are no exception. This recipe could be adapted by substituting split-peas or lentils for the chick-peas.

POULTRY AND GAME

Poultry and game are obvious choices for a low fat diet, as they are mostly very low in fat, and much of the fat they do contain is low in saturates. Chicken, always a favorite choice for family meals, is endlessly versatile and economical, and is well suited to low fat cooking methods. Turkey, also low fat, is now available in so many different cuts that it's almost interchangeable with chicken, and ground turkey can take the place of beef in healthy, savory bakes and pasta dishes. For a change, introduce game into family meals, as it is particularly low in saturated fat and just as simple to cook as chicken. Even high-fat poultry such as duck can be cooked in new ways to reduce fat – and add to the flavor.

JAMBALAYA

The perfect way to use up leftover cold meat – Jambalaya is a fast, easy-to-make fortifying meal for a hungry family.

INGREDIENTS

Serves 4

3 tbsp vegetable oil
1 onion, chopped
1 celery stalk, chopped
½ red bell pepper, chopped
2 cups long grain rice
4 cups chicken broth
1 tbsp tomato paste
3–4 shakes of Tabasco sauce
8oz cold roast chicken without skin
  and bone or lean pork, thickly sliced
4oz cooked sausage, such as chorizo or
  kabanos, sliced
¾ cup frozen peas

1 Heat the oil in a heavy saucepan, add the onion, celery and bell pepper. Cook gently until soft.

COOK'S TIP
Fish and shellfish are also good in a Jambalaya.

2 Add the rice, chicken broth, tomato paste and Tabasco sauce. Simmer uncovered for about 10 minutes.

3 Stir in the cold meat, sausage and peas and simmer for 5 minutes. Switch off the heat, cover and leave to stand for 5 minutes before serving.

NUTRITION NOTES

Per portion:

Energy	699Kcals/2936kJ
Fat	25.71g
Saturated fat	7.2g
Cholesterol	65.46mg
Fiber	1.95g

BROILED CHICKEN WITH HOT SALSA

This dish originates from
Mexico. Its hot and delicious
fruity flavors form the essence of
Tex-Mex cooking.

INGREDIENTS

Serves 4
4 chicken breasts without skin and
  bone, about 6oz each
pinch of celery salt and cayenne pepper
2 tbsp vegetable oil
fresh cilantro, to garnish
corn chips, to serve

For the salsa
10oz watermelon
6oz canteloupe melon
1 small red onion
1–2 green chilies
2 tbsp lime juice
4 tbsp chopped fresh cilantro
pinch of salt

NUTRITION NOTES	
Per portion:	
Energy	263Kcals/1106kJ
Fat	10.72g
Saturated fat	2.82g
Cholesterol	64.5mg
Fiber	0.72g

1 Preheat a moderate broiler. Slash the chicken breasts deeply to speed up the cooking time.

2 Season the chicken with celery salt and cayenne, brush with oil and broil for about 15 minutes.

3 For the salsa, remove the rind and seeds from the melons. Finely dice the flesh and put it into a bowl.

4 Finely chop the onion, split the chilies (discarding the seeds which contain most of the heat) and chop. Mix with the melon.

5 Add the lime juice and chopped cilantro, and season with a pinch of salt. Turn the salsa out into a small mixing bowl.

6 Arrange the broiled chicken on a plate and serve with the salsa and a handful of corn chips. Garnish with sprigs of cilantro.

> **COOK'S TIP**
> To capture the spirit of Tex-Mex food, cook the chicken over a barbecue and eat shaded from the hot summer sun.

MOROCCAN ROCK CORNISH HENS

Serves 4

1½ cups cooked long-grain rice
1 small onion, chopped finely
finely grated rind and juice of 1 lemon
2 tbsp chopped mint
3 tbsp chopped dried apricots
2 tbsp plain yogurt
2 tsp ground turmeric
2 tsp ground cumin
2 x 1lb Rock Cornish hens
salt and black pepper
lemon slices and mint sprigs, to garnish

1 Preheat the oven to 400°F. Mix together the rice, onion, lemon rind, mint, and apricots. Stir in half each of the lemon juice, yogurt, turmeric, cumin, and salt and pepper.

2 Stuff the hens with the rice mixture at the neck end only. Any spare stuffing can be served separately. Place the hens on a rack in a roasting pan.

3 Mix together the remaining lemon juice, yogurt, turmeric, and cumin, then brush this over the hens. Cover loosely with foil and roast in the oven for 30 minutes.

4 Remove the foil and roast for a further 15 minutes, or until golden brown and the juices run clear, not pink, when pierced.

5 Cut the hens in half with a sharp knife or poultry shears, and serve with the reserved rice. Garnish with lemon slices and fresh mint.

NUTRITION NOTES	
Per portion:	
Energy	219Kcals/919kJ
Fat	6.02g
Saturated fat	1.87g
Cholesterol	71.55mg
Fiber	1.12g

STICKY GINGER CHICKEN

Serves 4

2 tbsp lemon juice
2 tbsp brown sugar
1 tsp grated fresh ginger root
2 tsp soy sauce
8 chicken drumsticks, skinned
black pepper

NUTRITION NOTES	
Per portion:	
Energy	162Kcals/679kJ
Fat	5.58g
Saturated fat	1.84g
Cholesterol	73mg
Fiber	0.08g

1 Mix together the lemon juice, sugar, ginger, soy sauce, and pepper.

2 With a sharp knife, slash the chicken drumsticks about three times through the thickest part, then toss the chicken in the glaze.

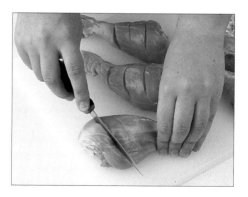

3 Cook the chicken under a broiler, or barbecue, turning occasionally and brushing with the glaze, until the chicken is golden and the juices run clear, not pink, when pierced. Serve on a bed of lettuce, with crusty bread.

STIR-FRIED SWEET AND SOUR CHICKEN

INGREDIENTS

Serves 4

10oz Chinese egg noodles
2 tbsp sunflower oil
3 scallions, chopped
1 garlic clove, crushed
1in piece fresh ginger root, peeled and
   grated
1 tsp hot paprika
1 tsp ground cilantro
3 chicken breasts without skin and
   bone, sliced
1 cup snow peas, topped
   and tailed
1¼ cups baby corn, halved
2¾ cups beansprouts
1 tbsp cornstarch
3 tbsp soy sauce
3 tbsp lemon juice
1 tbsp sugar
3 tbsp chopped fresh cilantro or
   scallion, to garnish

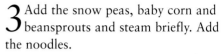

1 Bring a large saucepan of salted
water to a boil. Add the noodles
and cook according to the manufacturer's instructions. Drain and cover.

2 Heat the oil in a wok. Add the
scallions and cook over a gentle
heat. Mix in the garlic, ginger, paprika,
ground cilantro, and chicken, then stir-
fry for about 3–4 minutes.

3 Add the snow peas, baby corn and
beansprouts and steam briefly. Add
the noodles.

4 Combine the cornstarch, soy sauce,
lemon juice and sugar in a small
bowl. Add to the wok and simmer
briefly to thicken. Serve hot, garnished
with freshly chopped cilantro or
scallion tops.

NUTRITION NOTES

Per portion:

Energy	528Kcals/2218kJ
Fat	15.44g
Saturated fat	2.32g
Cholesterol	48.38mg
Fiber	2.01g

COOK'S TIP

Large wok lids are cumbersome
and can be difficult to store in a
small kitchen. Consider placing a
circle of waxed paper against the
food surface to keep cooking
juices in.

Be very careful when stir-frying
dishes. Timing is very important
and overcooking will ruin the
flavor. When correctly done, the
food should be crispy. The high
heat used in stir-frying will bring
out the natural juices of the
vegetables especially if fresh.

CHICKEN IN A CASHEW SAUCE

This chicken dish has a
deliciously thick and nutty sauce.

INGREDIENTS

Serves 4

2 onions
2 tbsp tomato paste
⅓ cup cashews
1½ tsp garam masala
1 garlic clove, crushed
1 tsp chili powder
1 tbsp lemon juice
¼ tsp turmeric
1 tsp salt
1 tbsp plain low fat yogurt
2 tbsp corn oil
1 tbsp chopped fresh cilantro
1 tbsp golden raisins
1lb chicken without skin and bone,
  cubed
2½ cups button mushrooms
1¼ cups water
sprig of cilantro, to garnish

NUTRITION NOTES

Per portion:
Energy	280Kcals/1176kJ
Fat	14.64g
Saturated fat	2.87g
Cholesterol	64.84mg

1 Cut the onions into quarters and
place in a food processor or blender
and process for about 1 minute.

2 Add the next five ingredients to the
processed onions.

3 Process all the ingredients in the
food processor for 1–1½ minutes
more to make a smooth paste.

4 In a saucepan, heat the oil, lower
the heat to medium and pour in the
spice mixture from the food processor.

5 Fry the mixture for 2 minutes,
lowering the heat if necessary.

6 Add the fresh cilantro, golden
raisins and chicken, and continue to
stir-fry for 1 minute more.

7 Add the mushrooms, pour in the
water and bring to a simmer. Cover
the pan and cook over a low heat for
about 10 minutes. Check that the
chicken is thoroughly cooked and the
sauce is thick. Cook longer if necessary.
Serve the chicken garnished with a
sprig of cilantro.

CHILI-CHICKEN COUSCOUS

Couscous is a very easy alternative to rice and makes a good base for all kinds of ingredients.

INGREDIENTS

Serves 4

2 cups couscous
4 cups boiling water
1 tsp olive oil
14oz chicken without skin and bone,
    diced
1 yellow bell pepper, seeded and sliced
2 large zucchini, sliced thickly
1 small green chili, thinly sliced, or
    1 tsp chili sauce
1 large tomato, diced
15oz can chick peas, drained
salt and black pepper
cilantro or parsley sprigs to garnish

1 Place couscous in a large bowl and pour over boiling water. Cover and let stand for 30 minutes.

2 Heat the oil in a large, nonstick pan and stir-fry the chicken quickly to seal, then reduce the heat.

3 Stir in the pepper, zucchini, and chili or sauce and cook for 10 minutes, until the vegetables are softened.

4 Stir in the tomato and chick peas, then add the couscous. Adjust the seasoning and stir over moderate heat until hot. Serve garnished with sprigs of fresh cilantro or parsley.

NUTRITION NOTES

Per portion:

Energy	363Kcals/1525kJ
Fat	8.09g
Saturated fat	1.68g
Cholesterol	57mg
Fiber	4.38g

TURKEY AND BEAN BAKE

INGREDIENTS

Serves 4

1 medium eggplant, thinly sliced
1 tbsp olive oil, for brushing
1 lb turkey breast, diced
1 medium onion, chopped
14oz can chopped tomatoes
15oz can red kidney beans, drained
1 tbsp paprika
1 tbsp fresh chopped thyme, or 1 tsp
    dried
1 tsp chili sauce
1½ cups plain yogurt
½ tsp ground nutmeg
salt and black pepper

1 Preheat the oven to 375°F. Arrange the eggplant in a colander and sprinkle with salt.

2 Leave the eggplant for 30 minutes, then rinse and pat dry. Brush a nonstick pan with oil and cook the eggplant in batches, turning once, until golden.

3 Remove the eggplant, add the turkey and onion to the pan, then cook until lightly browned. Stir in the tomatoes, beans, paprika, thyme, chili sauce, and salt and pepper. In a separate bowl, mix together the yogurt and ground nutmeg.

4 Layer the meat and eggplant in an ovenproof dish, finishing with eggplant. Spread over the yogurt and bake for 50–60 minutes, until golden.

NUTRITION NOTES

Per portion:

Energy	370Kcals/1555kJ
Fat	13.72g
Saturated fat	5.81g
Cholesterol	66.5mg
Fiber	7.38g

SPICY MASALA CHICKEN

These chicken pieces are broiled and have a sweet-and-sour taste. They can be served cold with a salad and rice, or hot with mashed potatoes.

INGREDIENTS

Serves 6
12 *chicken thighs without skin*
6 *tbsp lemon juice*
1 *tsp grated fresh ginger root*
1 *garlic clove, crushed*
1 *tsp crushed dried red chilies*
1 *tsp salt*
1 *tsp soft brown sugar*
2 *tbsp clear honey*
2 *tbsp chopped fresh cilantro*
1 *green chili, finely chopped*
2 *tbsp sunflower oil*
sliced chili, to garnish

1 Prick the chicken thighs with a fork, rinse, pat dry and set aside in a large bowl.

2 In a large mixing bowl, mix together the lemon juice, ginger, garlic, crushed dried red chilies, salt, sugar and honey.

3 Transfer the chicken thighs to the spice mixture and coat well. Set aside for about 45 minutes.

4 Preheat the broiler to medium. Add the fresh cilantro and chopped green chili to the chicken thighs and place them on a flameproof dish.

5 Pour any remaining marinade over the chicken and baste with the oil, using a pastry brush.

6 Broil the chicken thighs under the preheated broiler for about 15–20 minutes, turning and basting occasionally, until cooked through and browned.

7 Transfer to a serving dish and garnish with the sliced chili.

NUTRITION NOTES	
Per portion:	
Energy	189Kcals/795kJ
Fat	9.2g
Saturated fat	2.31g
Cholesterol	73mg

TANDOORI CHICKEN

This popular Indian chicken dish is traditionally cooked in a clay oven called a tandoor. Although the authentic tandoori flavor is very difficult to achieve in conventional ovens, this version still makes a very tasty dish.

INGREDIENTS

Serves 4

4 chicken quarters without skin
¼ cup plain low fat yogurt
1 tsp garam masala
1 tsp grated fresh ginger root
1 garlic clove, crushed
1½ tsp chili powder
¼ tsp turmeric
1 tsp ground cilantro
1 tbsp lemon juice
1 tsp salt
a few drops of red food coloring,
  (optional)
2 tbsp corn oil

For the garnish
mixed salad leaves
lime slices
chilies
tomato quarters

1 Rinse and pat dry the chicken quarters. Make two slits into the flesh of each piece, place in a dish and set aside.

2 Mix together the yogurt, garam masala, ginger, garlic, chili powder, turmeric, ground cilantro, lemon juice, salt, red coloring, if using, and oil, and beat so that all the ingredients are mixed together well.

3 Cover the chicken quarters with the spice mixture and leave to marinate for about 3 hours.

4 Preheat the oven to 475°F. Transfer the chicken pieces to an ovenproof dish or baking pan.

5 Bake in the preheated oven for about 20–25 minutes or until the chicken is cooked right through and browned on top.

6 Remove from the oven, transfer on to a serving dish, and garnish with the salad leaves, lime and tomato.

NUTRITION NOTES	
Per portion:	
Energy	242Kcals/1018kJ
Fat	10.64g
Saturated fat	2.74g
Cholesterol	81.9mg

TURKEY PASTITSIO

A traditional Greek pastitsio is a rich, high-fat dish made with ground beef, but this lighter version is just as tasty.

INGREDIENTS

Serves 4–6

1 lb lean ground turkey
1 large onion, finely chopped
4 tbsp tomato paste
1 cup red wine or broth
1 tsp ground cinnamon
2½ cups macaroni
1¼ cups skim milk
2 tbsp sunflower margarine
3 tbsp flour
1 tsp ground nutmeg
2 tomatoes, sliced
4 tbsp whole-wheat bread crumbs
salt and black pepper
green salad, to serve

1 Preheat the oven to 425°F. Cook the turkey and chopped onion in a nonstick pan without fat, stirring until lightly browned.

2 Stir in the tomato paste, red wine or broth, and cinnamon. Season, then cover and simmer for 5 minutes.

3 Cook the macaroni in boiling, salted water until just tender, then drain. Layer with the meat mixture in a wide ovenproof dish.

4 Place the milk, margarine, and flour in a saucepan and whisk over a moderate heat until thickened and smooth. Add the nutmeg, and salt and pepper to taste.

5 Pour the sauce evenly over the pasta and meat. Arrange the tomato slices on top and sprinkle lines of bread crumbs over the surface.

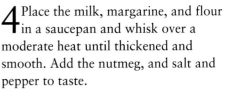

6 Bake for 30–35 minutes, or until golden brown and bubbling. Serve hot, with a green salad.

NUTRITION NOTES

Per portion:

Energy	566Kcals/2382kJ
Fat	8.97g
Saturated fat	1.76g
Cholesterol	57.06mg
Fiber	4.86g

TUSCAN CHICKEN

This simple peasant casserole has all the flavors of traditional Tuscan ingredients. The wine can be replaced by chicken broth.

INGREDIENTS

Serves 4
8 chicken thighs, skinned
1 tsp olive oil
1 medium onion, sliced thinly
2 red bell peppers, seeded and sliced
1 garlic clove, crushed
1¼ cups puréed tomatoes
⅔ cup dry white wine
large sprig fresh oregano, or 1 tsp dried
*   oregano*
14oz can cannelini beans, drained
3 tbsp fresh bread crumbs
salt and black pepper

1 Cook the chicken in the oil in a nonstick or heavy pan until golden brown. Remove and keep hot. Add the onion and bell peppers to the pan and gently sauté until softened, but not brown. Stir in the garlic.

2 Add the chicken, tomatoes, wine, and oregano. Season well, bring to a boil, then cover the pan tightly.

NUTRITION NOTES

Per portion:
Energy	248Kcals/1045kJ
Fat	7.53g
Saturated fat	2.06g
Cholesterol	73mg
Fiber	4.03g

3 Lower the heat and simmer gently, stirring occasionally for 30–35 minutes or until the chicken is tender and the juices run clear, not pink, when pierced with the point of a knife.

4 Stir in the cannelini beans and simmer for 5 minutes more, until heated through. Sprinkle with the bread crumbs and cook under a broiler until golden brown.

MANDARIN SESAME DUCK

Duck is a high-fat meat but it is possible to get rid of a good proportion of the fat cooked in this way. (If you remove the skin completely, the meat can be dry.) For a special occasion, duck breasts are a good choice, but they are more expensive.

— INGREDIENTS —

Serves 4

4 duck legs or boneless breasts
2 tbsp light soy sauce
3 tbsp clear honey
1 tbsp sesame seeds
4 mandarin oranges or tangerines
1 tsp cornstarch
salt and black pepper

1 Preheat the oven to 180°C/350°F/ Gas 4. Prick the duck skin all over. Slash the breast skin diagonally at intervals with a sharp knife.

2 Place the duck on a rack in a roasting pan and roast for 1 hour. Mix 1 tbsp soy sauce with 2 tbsp honey and brush over the duck. Sprinkle with sesame seeds. Roast for 15–20 minutes, until golden brown.

3 Meanwhile, grate the rind from one mandarin and squeeze the juice from two. Mix in the cornstarch, then stir in the remaining soy sauce and honey. Heat, stirring, until thickened and clear. Season. Peel and slice the remaining mandarins. Serve the duck, with the mandarin slices and the sauce.

— NUTRITION NOTES —

Per portion:

Energy	624Kcals/2621kJ
Fat	48.63g
Saturated fat	12.99g
Cholesterol	256mg
Fiber	0.95g

MINTY YOGURT CHICKEN

— INGREDIENTS —

Serves 4

8 chicken thighs, skinned
1 tbsp clear honey
2 tbsp lime or lemon juice
2 tbsp plain yogurt
4 tbsp chopped fresh mint
salt and black pepper

1 Slash the chicken flesh at intervals with a sharp knife. Place in a bowl.

2 Mix the lime or honey, lemon juice, yogurt, seasoning and half the mint.

3 Spoon the marinade over the chicken and leave to marinate for 30 minutes. Line a broiler pan with foil and cook the chicken under a broiler until thoroughly cooked and golden brown, turning the chicken occasionally during cooking.

4 Sprinkle with the remaining mint. Serve with potatoes and tomato salad.

— NUTRITION NOTES —

Per portion:

Energy	171Kcals/719kJ
Fat	6.74g
Saturated fat	2.23g
Cholesterol	97.90mg
Fiber	0.01g

TURKEY SPIRALS

These little spirals may look difficult, but they're very simple to make, and a very good way to pep up plain turkey.

INGREDIENTS

Serves 4

*4 thinly sliced turkey breasts, about
   3½oz each
4 tsp tomato paste
½ cup large basil leaves
1 garlic clove, crushed
1 tbsp skim milk
2 tbsp whole-wheat flour
salt and black pepper
fresh tomato sauce and pasta with fresh
   basil, to serve*

1 Place the turkey steaks on a board. If too thick, flatten them slightly by beating with a rolling pin.

2 Spread each turkey breast with tomato paste, then top with a few leaves of basil, a little crushed garlic, and salt and pepper.

3 Roll up firmly around the filling and secure with a toothpick. Brush with milk and sprinkle with flour to coat lightly.

4 Place the spirals on a foil-lined broiler pan. Cook under a broiler for 15–20 minutes, turning them occasionally, until thoroughly cooked. Serve hot, sliced with a spoonful or two of fresh tomato sauce and pasta, sprinkled with fresh basil.

> COOK'S TIP
> When flattening the turkey breasts with a rolling pin, place them between two sheets of plastic wrap.

NUTRITION NOTES

Per portion:

Energy	123Kcals/518kJ
Fat	1.21g
Saturated fat	0.36g
Cholesterol	44.17mg
Fiber	0.87g

CARIBBEAN CHICKEN KABOBS

These kabobs have a rich, sunshine Caribbean flavor and the marinade keeps them moist without the need for oil. Serve with a colorful salad and rice.

INGREDIENTS

Serves 4

1¼ lb boneless chicken breasts, skinned
finely grated rind of 1 lime
2 tbsp lime juice
1 tbsp rum or sherry
1 tbsp brown sugar
1 tsp ground cinnamon
2 mangoes, peeled and cubed
rice and salad, to serve

1 Cut the chicken into bite-sized chunks and place in a bowl with the lime rind and juice, rum, sugar, and cinnamon. Toss well, cover, and leave to marinate for 1 hour.

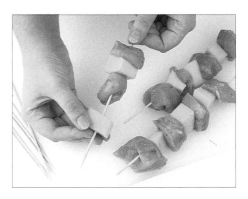

2 Save the juices and thread the chicken onto four wooden skewers, alternating with the mango cubes.

3 Cook the skewers under a broiler, or barbecue, for 8–10 minutes, turning occasionally and basting with the juices, until the chicken is tender and golden brown. Serve at once, with rice and salad.

COOK'S TIP
The rum or sherry adds a lovely rich flavor, but it is optional so can be omitted if you prefer to avoid the added alcohol.

NUTRITION NOTES

Per portion:

Energy	218Kcals/918kJ
Fat	4.17g
Saturated fat	1.33g
Cholesterol	53.75mg
Fiber	2.26g

OATMEAL-COATED CHICKEN WITH SAGE

Oatmeal makes a good coating for savory foods, and offers a good way to add extra fiber.

INGREDIENTS

Serves 4

3 tbsp skim milk
2 tsp plain mustard
½ cup oatmeal
3 tbsp chopped sage leaves
8 chicken thighs or drumsticks, skinned
½ cup low fat fromage frais
1 tsp whole-grain mustard
salt and black pepper
fresh sage leaves, to garnish

1 Preheat the oven to 400°F. Mix together the milk and plain mustard.

2 Mix the oatmeal with 2 tbsp of the sage and the seasoning on a plate. Brush the chicken with the milk and press into the oatmeal to coat.

3 Place the chicken on a baking sheet and bake for about 40 minutes, or until the juices run clear, not pink, when pierced through the thickest part.

4 Meanwhile, mix together the low fat fromage frais, mustard, remaining sage and seasoning, then serve with the chicken. Garnish the chicken with fresh sage and serve hot or cold.

COOK'S TIP
If fresh sage is not available, choose another fresh herb such as thyme or parsley, instead of using a dried alternative.

NUTRITION NOTES

Per portion:

Energy	214Kcals/898kJ
Fat	6.57g
Saturated fat	1.81g
Cholesterol	64.64mg
Fiber	0.74g

CHICKEN IN CREAMY ORANGE SAUCE

This sauce is deceptively creamy – in fact it is made with low fat fromage frais, which is virtually fat-free. The brandy adds a richer flavor, but is optional – omit it if you prefer and use orange juice alone.

INGREDIENTS

Serves 4
8 chicken thighs or drumsticks, skinned
3 tbsp brandy
1¼ cups orange juice
3 scallions, chopped
2 tsp cornstarch
6 tbsp low fat fromage frais
salt and black pepper

1 Cook the chicken pieces without fat in a nonstick or heavy pan, turning until evenly browned.

2 Stir in the brandy, orange juice and scallions. Bring to a boil, then cover and simmer for 15 minutes, or until the chicken is tender and the juices run clear, not pink, when pierced.

3 Blend the cornstarch with a little water then mix into the fromage frais. Stir this into the sauce and stir over moderate heat until boiling.

4 Adjust the seasoning and serve with boiled rice or pasta and green salad.

COOK'S TIP
Cornstarch stabilizes the fromage frais and helps prevent it curdling.

NUTRITION NOTES

Per portion:
Energy	227Kcals/951kJ
Fat	6.77g
Saturated fat	2.23g
Cholesterol	87.83mg
Fiber	0.17g

PHEASANT WITH APPLES

Pheasant is worth buying as it is low in fat, full of flavor, and never dry when cooked like this.

INGREDIENTS

Serves 4

1 pheasant
2 small onions, quartered
3 celery stalks, thickly sliced
2 red eating apples, thickly sliced
½ cup broth
1 tbsp clear honey
2 tbsp Worcestershire sauce
ground nutmeg
2 tbsp toasted hazelnuts
salt and black pepper

1 Preheat the oven to 350°F. Sauté the pheasant without fat in a nonstick pan, turning occasionally until golden. Remove and keep hot.

2 Sauté the onions and celery in the pan to brown lightly. Spoon into a casserole and place the pheasant on top. Tuck the apple slices around it.

3 Spoon over the broth, honey, and Worcestershire sauce. Sprinkle with nutmeg, salt and pepper, cover, and bake for 1¼ –1½ hours or until tender. Sprinkle with nuts and serve hot.

NUTRITION NOTES

Per portion:

Energy	387Kcals/1624kJ
Fat	16.97g
Saturated fat	4.28g
Cholesterol	126mg
Fiber	2.72g

CIDER BAKED RABBIT

Rabbit is a low fat meat and an economical choice for family meals. Chicken pieces may be used as an alternative.

INGREDIENTS

Serves 4

1 lb rabbit pieces
1 tbsp all-purpose flour
1 tsp dry mustard
3 medium leeks, thickly sliced
1 cup dry cider
2 sprigs rosemary
salt and black pepper
fresh rosemary, to garnish

1 Preheat the oven to 350°F. Place the rabbit pieces in a bowl and sprinkle over the flour and mustard. Toss to coat evenly.

2 Arrange the rabbit in one layer in a wide casserole. Blanch the leeks in boiling water, then drain and add to the casserole.

3 Add the cider, rosemary, and seasoning, cover, then bake for 1–1¼ hours, or until the rabbit is tender. Garnish with fresh rosemary, and serve with baked potatoes and vegetables.

NUTRITION NOTES

Per portion:

Energy	162Kcals/681kJ
Fat	4.22g
Saturated fat	1.39g
Cholesterol	62.13mg
Fiber	1.27g

CHINESE-STYLE CHICKEN SALAD

INGREDIENTS

Serves 4

*4 boneless chicken breasts, about
  6oz each*
4 tbsp dark soy sauce
pinch of Chinese five-spice powder
a good squeeze of lemon juice
*½ cucumber, peeled and cut into
  matchsticks*
1 tsp salt
3 tbsp sunflower oil
2 tbsp sesame oil
1 tbsp sesame seeds
2 tbsp dry sherry
2 carrots, cut into matchsticks
8 scallions, shredded
1 cup beansprouts

For the sauce
4 tbsp crunchy peanut butter
2 tsp lemon juice
2 tsp sesame oil
¼ tsp hot chili powder
1 scallion, finely chopped

1 Place the chicken portions in a large saucepan and just cover with water. Add 1 tbsp of the soy sauce, the Chinese five-spice powder and lemon juice, cover and bring to a boil, then simmer for about 20 minutes.

2 Meanwhile, place the cucumber matchsticks in a colander, sprinkle with the salt and cover with a plate with a weight on top. Leave to drain for about 30 minutes – set the colander in a bowl or on a deep plate to catch any drips that may fall.

3 Lift out the poached chicken with a slotted spoon and leave until cool enough to handle. Remove and discard the skins and bash the chicken lightly with a rolling pin to loosen the fibers. Slice into thin strips and reserve.

4 Heat the oils in a large frying pan or wok. Add the sesame seeds, fry for 30 seconds and then stir in the remaining 3 tbsp soy sauce and the sherry. Add the carrots and stir-fry for about 2–3 minutes, until just tender. Remove the wok or pan from the heat and reserve until required.

5 Rinse the cucumber well, pat dry with paper towel and place in a bowl. Add the scallions, beansprouts, cooked carrots, pan juices and shredded chicken, and mix together. Transfer to a shallow dish. Cover and chill for about 1 hour, turning the mixture in the juices once or twice.

6 For the sauce, cream the peanut butter with the lemon juice, sesame oil and chili powder, adding a little hot water to form a paste, then stir in the scallion. Arrange the chicken mixture on a serving dish and serve with the peanut sauce.

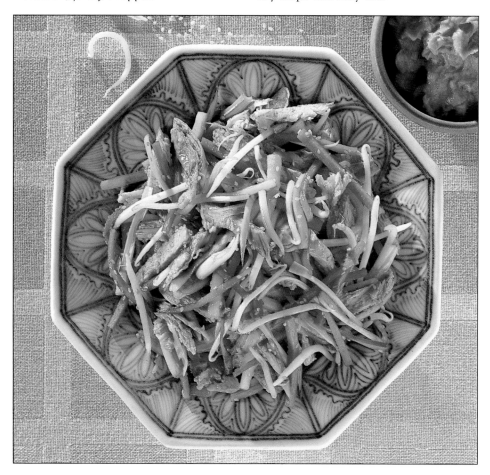

NUTRITION NOTES	
Per portion:	
Energy	534Kcals/2241kJ
Fat	36.86g
Saturated fat	4.96g
Cholesterol	68.8mg
Fiber	2.91g

CHICKEN BIRYANI

INGREDIENTS

Serves 4

1½ cups basmati rice, rinsed
½ tsp salt
5 whole cardamom pods
2–3 whole cloves
1 cinnamon stick
3 tbsp sunflower oil
3 onions, sliced
1½lb chicken breasts without skin and
    bone, cubed
¼ tsp ground cloves
5 cardamom pods, seeds removed
    and ground
¼ tsp hot chili powder
1 tsp ground cumin
1 tsp ground cilantro
½ tsp ground black pepper
3 garlic cloves, finely chopped
1 tsp finely chopped fresh
    ginger root
juice of 1 lemon
4 tomatoes, sliced
2 tbsp chopped fresh cilantro
⅔ cup plain low fat yogurt
½ tsp saffron strands soaked in 2 tsp
    hot skim milk
3 tbsp toasted sliced almonds, fresh
    cilantro leaves, to garnish
plain low fat yogurt, to serve

2 Heat the oil in a frying pan and fry the onions for about 8 minutes, until browned. Add the chicken followed by all the ground spices, the garlic, ginger and lemon juice. Stir-fry for 5 minutes more.

NUTRITION NOTES	
Per portion:	
Energy	650Kcals/2730kJ
Fat	21.43g
Saturated fat	3.62g
Cholesterol	74.11mg
Fiber	2.95g

3 Transfer the chicken mixture to an ovenproof casserole and lay the tomatoes on top. Sprinkle over the fresh cilantro, spoon over the yogurt, and top with the drained rice.

4 Drizzle the saffron strands and milk over the rice and pour over ⅔ cup of water.

1 Preheat the oven to 375°F. Bring a saucepan of water to a boil and add the rice, salt, cardamom pods, cloves and cinnamon stick. Boil for about 2 minutes and then drain, leaving the whole spices in the rice.

5 Cover with a tight fitting lid and bake in the oven for about 1 hour. Transfer to a warmed serving platter and remove the whole spices from the rice. Garnish with toasted almonds, fresh cilantro leaves and serve with a little yogurt.

STIR-FRIED TURKEY WITH SNOW PEAS

A quick and easy dish served
with saffron rice.

INGREDIENTS

Serves 4
2 tbsp sesame oil
6 tbsp lemon juice
1 garlic clove, crushed
½in piece fresh ginger root, grated
1 tsp clear honey
1lb lean turkey fillets, cut
    into strips
1 cup snow peas, trimmed
2 tbsp peanut oil
⅓ cup cashews
6 scallions, cut into strips
8oz can water chestnuts, drained and
    thinly sliced
pinch of salt
saffron rice, to serve

1 Mix together the sesame oil, lemon
juice, garlic, ginger and honey in a
shallow non-metallic dish. Add the
turkey and mix well. Cover and leave
to marinate for about 3–4 hours.

2 Blanch the snow peas in boiling
salted water for 1 minute. Drain
and refresh under cold running water.

3 Drain the marinade from the turkey
strips and reserve the marinade.
Heat the peanut oil in a wok or large
frying pan, add the cashews, and stir-
fry for about 1–2 minutes.

NUTRITION NOTES	
Per portion:	
Energy	311Kcals/1307kJ
Fat	18.51g
Saturated fat	2.9g
Cholesterol	55.12mg

4 Remove the cashews from the wok
or frying pan using a slotted spoon
and set aside.

5 Add the turkey and stir-fry for
about 3–4 minutes, until golden
brown. Add the snow peas, scallions
and water chestnuts with the reserved
marinade. Cook until the turkey is very
tender and the sauce is bubbling and
hot. Add salt to taste, then stir in the
cashews and serve the dish at once with
saffron rice.

HOT CHICKEN CURRY

This curry has a flavorful thick sauce, and includes red and green bell peppers for extra color. Serve with whole-wheat chapatis or plain boiled rice.

INGREDIENTS

Serves 4

2 tbsp corn oil
¼ tsp fenugreek seeds
¼ tsp onion seeds
2 onions, chopped
1 garlic clove, crushed
½ tsp grated fresh ginger root
1 tsp ground cilantro
1 tsp chili powder
1 tsp salt
14oz can tomatoes
2 tbsp lemon juice
12oz chicken without skin and
    bone, cubed
2 tbsp chopped fresh cilantro
3 green chilies, chopped
½ red bell pepper, cut into chunks
½ green bell pepper, cut into chunks
fresh cilantro leaves, to garnish

1 Heat the oil in a medium saucepan, and fry the fenugreek and onion seeds until they turn a shade darker. Add the onions, garlic and ginger and fry for about 5 minutes until the onions are golden. Lower the heat to very low.

COOK'S TIP
For a milder version of this delicious curry, simply omit some or all of the fresh green chilies.

2 Meanwhile, in a separate bowl, mix together the ground cilantro, chili powder, salt, tomatoes and lemon juice.

3 Pour this mixture into the pan and turn up the heat to medium. Stir-fry for about 3 minutes.

NUTRITION NOTES

Per portion:
Energy	205Kcals/861kJ
Fat	9.83g
Saturated fat	2.03g
Cholesterol	48.45mg

4 Add the chicken and stir-fry for about 5–7 minutes. Take care not to overcook the chicken.

5 Add the fresh cilantro, green chilies and the sliced bell peppers. Lower the heat, cover, and simmer for about 10 minutes until cooked. Serve hot, garnished with fresh cilantro leaves.

FISH AND SEAFOOD

Fish is ideally designed for healthy, quick family meals. Most types of fish are very low in fat and high in protein, and even oily fish is high in essential fatty acids. Unlike meat, fish never needs long, slow cooking to tenderize it, so dinner can be on the table in less than half an hour! Tempt reluctant fish eaters with wonderful exotic flavors – a spicy Moroccan Fish Tagine perhaps, or a hearty Cod Creole to pep up the taste buds. Fussy young fish-eaters are sure to clean their plate of Fish Balls in Tomato Sauce or Tuna and Corn Fish Cakes, or will even try mackerel if it is presented without risk of bones, on fun-to-eat kabobs.

SHRIMP WITH VEGETABLES

This is a light and nutritious dish. It is excellent served either on a bed of lettuce leaves, with plain boiled rice or whole-wheat chapatis for a healthy meal.

INGREDIENTS

Serves 4
2 tbsp chopped fresh cilantro
1 tsp salt
2 green chilies, seeded if required
3 tbsp lemon juice
2 tbsp vegetable oil
20 cooked jumbo shrimp, peeled
1 zucchini, thickly sliced
1 onion, cut into 8 chunks
8 cherry tomatoes
8 baby corn
mixed salad leaves, to serve

NUTRITION NOTES

Per portion:
Energy   109Kcals/458kJ
Fat   6.47g
Saturated fat   0.85g
Cholesterol   29.16mg

1 Place the chopped cilantro, salt, green chilies, lemon juice and oil in a food processor or blender and process for a few seconds.

2 Remove the chili paste from the food processor or blender and transfer to a mixing bowl.

3 Add the peeled shrimp to the paste and stir to make sure that all the shrimp are well coated. Set aside to marinate for about 30 minutes.

4 Preheat the broiler to very hot, then turn the heat down to medium.

5 Arrange the vegetables and shrimp alternately on four skewers. When all the skewers are ready, place them under the preheated broiler for 5–7 minutes until cooked and browned.

6 Serve immediately on a bed of mixed salad leaves.

COOK'S TIP
Jumbo shrimp are a luxury, but worth choosing for a very special dinner party. For a more economical variation, substitute the jumbo shrimp with 2½ cups ordinary shrimp.

BROILED FISH FILLETS

Fish can be broiled beautifully without sacrificing any flavor. This recipe uses a minimum amount of oil to baste the fish.

INGREDIENTS

Serves 4
4 flatfish fillets, such as plaice, sole or flounder, about 4oz each
1 garlic clove, crushed
1 tsp garam masala
1 tsp chili powder
¼ tsp turmeric
½ tsp salt
1 tbsp finely chopped fresh cilantro, or parsley
1 tbsp vegetable oil
2 tbsp lemon juice

1 Line a flameproof dish or broiler tray with foil. Rinse and pat dry the fish fillets and put them on the foil-lined dish or tray.

2 In a small bowl, mix together the garlic, garam masala, chili powder, turmeric, salt, fresh cilantro or parsley, oil and lemon juice.

3 Using a pastry brush, baste the fish fillets evenly all over with the spice and lemon juice mixture.

COOK'S TIP
Although frozen fish can be used for this dish always try to buy fresh. It is more flavorsome.

4 Preheat the broiler to very hot, then lower the heat to medium. Broil the fillets for about 10 minutes, turning as necessary and basting occasionally, until they are cooked right through.

5 Serve immediately with an attractive garnish. This could include grated carrot, tomato quarters and lime slices, if you wish.

NUTRITION NOTES

Per portion:	
Energy	143Kcals/599kJ
Fat	5.63g
Saturated fat	0.84g
Cholesterol	47.25mg

CRUNCHY-TOPPED COD

Colorful and quick to cook, this is ideal for weekday meals.

INGREDIENTS

Serves 4

4 pieces cod fillet, about 4oz each, skinned
2 medium tomatoes, sliced
1 cup fresh whole-wheat bread crumbs
2 tbsp chopped fresh parsley
finely grated rind and juice of ½ lemon
1 tsp sunflower oil
salt and black pepper

1 Preheat the oven to 400ºF. Arrange the cod fillets in a wide, ovenproof dish.

2 Arrange the tomato slices on top. Mix together the bread crumbs, fresh parsley, lemon rind and juice, and the oil with seasoning to taste.

3 Spoon the crumb mixture evenly over the fish, then bake for 15–20 minutes. Serve hot.

NUTRITION NOTES	
Per portion:	
Energy	130Kcals/546kJ
Fat	2.06g
Saturated fat	0.32g
Cholesterol	52.9mg
Fiber	1.4g

SPECIAL FISH PIE

This fish pie is colorful, healthy, and best of all very easy to make. For a more economical version, omit the shrimp and replace with more fish fillet.

INGREDIENTS

Serves 4

12oz haddock fillet, skinned
2 tbsp cornstarch
4oz cooked, peeled shrimp
7oz can corn kernels, drained
¾ cup frozen peas
⅔ cup skim milk
⅔ cup low fat fromage frais
1½ cups fresh whole-wheat bread crumbs
½ cup shredded low fat Cheddar cheese
salt and black pepper

1 Preheat the oven to 375ºF. Cut the haddock into bite-sized pieces and toss in cornstarch.

2 Place the fish, shrimp, corn, and peas in an ovenproof dish. Beat together the milk, fromage frais, and seasonings, then pour into the dish.

3 Mix together the bread crumbs and shredded cheese, then spoon evenly over the top. Bake for 25–30 minutes, or until golden brown. Serve hot, with fresh vegetables.

NUTRITION NOTES	
Per portion:	
Energy	290Kcals/1218kJ
Fat	4.87g
Saturated fat	2.1g
Cholesterol	63.91mg
Fiber	2.61g

HADDOCK AND BROCCOLI CHOWDER

A warming main-meal soup for hearty appetites.

INGREDIENTS

Serves 4

4 scallions, sliced
1 lb new potatoes, diced
1¼ cups fish broth or water
1¼ cups skim milk
1 bay leaf
2 cups broccoli florets, sliced
1 lb smoked haddock fillets, skinned
7oz can corn kernels, drained
black pepper
chopped scallions, to garnish

1 Place the scallions and potatoes in a large saucepan and add the broth, milk, and bay leaf. Bring the soup to a boil, then cover the pan and simmer for 10 minutes.

2 Add the broccoli to the pan. Cut the fish into bite-sized chunks and add to the pan with the corn kernels.

3 Season the soup well with black pepper, then cover the pan and simmer for 5 minutes more, or until the fish is cooked through. Remove the bay leaf and scatter over the scallions. Serve hot, with crusty bread.

COOK'S TIP
When new potatoes are not available, old ones can be used, but choose a waxy variety that will not disintegrate.

NUTRITION NOTES

Per portion:

Energy	268Kcals/1124kJ
Fat	2.19g
Saturated fat	0.27g
Cholesterol	57.75mg
Fiber	3.36g

MOROCCAN FISH TAGINE

Tagine is actually the name of the large Moroccan cooking pot used for this type of cooking, but you can use an ordinary casserole intead.

— INGREDIENTS —

Serves 4
2 garlic cloves, crushed
2 tbsp ground cumin
2 tbsp paprika
1 small red chili (optional)
2 tbsp tomato paste
4 tbsp lemon juice
4 whiting or cod steaks, about 6oz each
12oz tomatoes, sliced
2 green bell peppers, seeded and
    thinly sliced
salt and black pepper
chopped fresh cilantro, to garnish

1 Mix together the garlic, cumin, paprika, chili, tomato paste and lemon juice. Spread this mixture over the fish, then cover and chill for about 30 minutes to let the flavor penetrate.

2 Preheat the oven to 400°F. Arrange half of the tomatoes and peppers in a baking dish.

3 Cover with the fish, in one layer, then arrange the remaining tomatoes and bell pepper on top. Cover the baking dish with foil and bake for about 45 minutes, until the fish is cooked through. Sprinkle with chopped cilantro and serve.

COOK'S TIP
If you are preparing this dish for a dinner party, it can be assembled completely and stored in the fridge, ready for baking when needed.

— NUTRITION NOTES —

Per portion:
Energy	203Kcals/855kJ
Fat	3.34g
Saturated fat	0.29g
Cholesterol	80.5mg
Fiber	2.48g

Seafood Pilaf

This all-in-one-pan main course is a satisfying meal for any day of the week. For a special meal, substitute dry white wine for the orange juice.

Ingredients

Serves 4
2 tsp olive oil
1¼ cups long-grain rice
1 tsp ground turmeric
1 red bell pepper, seeded and diced
1 small onion, finely chopped
2 medium zucchini, sliced
2 cups button mushrooms, halved
1½ cups fish or chicken broth
⅔ cup orange juice
12oz white fish fillets
12 fresh mussels in the shell (or cooked shelled mussels)
salt and ground black pepper
grated rind of 1 orange, to garnish

1 Heat the oil in a large, nonstick pan and sauté the rice and turmeric over low heat for about 1 minute.

2 Add the pepper, onion, zucchini, and mushrooms. Stir in the broth and orange juice. Bring to a boil.

3 Reduce the heat and add the fish. Cover and simmer gently for about 15 minutes, until the rice is tender and the liquid absorbed. Stir in the mussels and heat thoroughly. Adjust the seasoning, sprinkle with orange rind, and serve hot.

Nutrition Notes

Per portion:
Energy	370Kcals/1555kJ
Fat	3.84g
Saturated fat	0.64g
Cholesterol	61.25mg
Fiber	2.08g

Salmon Pasta with Parsley Sauce

Ingredients

Serves 4
1 lb salmon fillet, skinned
3 cups pasta, such as penne or twists
6oz cherry tomatoes, halved
⅔ cup low fat crème fraîche
3 tbsp finely chopped parsley
finely grated rind of ½ orange
salt and black pepper

Nutrition Notes

Per portion:
Energy	452Kcals/1902kJ
Fat	17.4g
Saturated fat	5.36g
Cholesterol	65.63mg
Fiber	2.56g

1 Cut the salmon into bite-sized pieces, arrange on a heatproof plate, and cover with foil.

2 Bring a large pan of salted water to the boil, add the pasta, and return to a boil. Place the plate of salmon on top and simmer for 10–12 minutes, until the pasta and salmon are cooked.

3 Drain the pasta and toss with the tomatoes and salmon. Mix together the crème fraîche, parsley, orange rind, and pepper to taste, then toss into the salmon and pasta and serve hot or cold.

STUFFED SOLE ROLLS

Sole fillets are a good choice because they are mild in flavor, easy to cook, and free of bones. Have your fillets prepared when you buy them.

INGREDIENTS

Serves 4

1 medium zucchini, grated
2 medium carrots, grated
4 tbsp fresh whole-wheat bread crumbs
1 tbsp lime or lemon juice
4 sole fillets
salt and black pepper

1 Preheat the oven to 400°F. Mix together the grated carrots and zucchini. Stir in the bread crumbs, lime juice, and seasoning to taste.

2 Lay the fish fillets skin side up and divide the stuffing between them, spreading it evenly.

3 Roll up to enclose the stuffing and place in an ovenproof dish. Cover and bake for about 30 minutes, or until the fish flakes easily. Serve hot with new potatoes.

COOK'S TIP
This recipe creates its own delicious juices, but for an extra sauce, stir chopped fresh parsley into a little low fat fromage frais and serve with the fish.

NUTRITION NOTES

Per portion:

Energy	158Kcals/665kJ
Fat	3.22g
Saturated fat	0.56g
Cholesterol	50.4mg
Fiber	1.94g

MACKEREL KABOBS WITH PARSLEY DRESSING

Oily fish such as mackerel are
ideal for broiling as they cook
quickly and need no extra oil.

INGREDIENTS

Serves 4
1 lb mackerel fillets
finely grated rind and juice of 1 lemon
3 tbsp chopped fresh parsley
12 cherry tomatoes
8 pitted ripe olives
salt and black pepper

1 Cut the fish into 1½in chunks and
place in a bowl with half the lemon
rind and juice, half of the parsley and
some seasoning. Cover the bowl and
leave to marinate for 30 minutes.

2 Thread the chunks of fish onto eight
long wooden or metal skewers,
alternating them with the cherry
tomatoes and olives. Cook the kabobs
under a hot broiler for 3–4 minutes,
turning the kabobs occasionally, until
the fish is cooked.

3 Mix the remaining lemon rind and
juice with the remaining parsley in a
small bowl, then season to taste with
salt and pepper. Spoon the dressing
over the kabobs and serve hot, with
plain boiled rice or noodles and a leafy
green salad.

COOK'S TIP
When using wooden or bamboo
kabob skewers, soak them first in a
bowl of cold water for a few minutes to help prevent them burning.

NUTRITION NOTES

Per portion:
Energy   268Kcals/1126kJ
Fat   19.27g
Saturated fat   4.5g
Cholesterol   61.88mg
Fiber   1g

FISH FILLETS WITH A CHILI SAUCE

Fish fillets, marinated with fresh cilantro and lemon juice, then broiled and served with a chili sauce, are delicious accompanied with saffron rice.

INGREDIENTS

Serves 4

4 flatfish fillets, such as plaice, sole or flounder, about 4oz each
2 tbsp lemon juice
1 tbsp finely chopped fresh cilantro
1 tbsp vegetable oil
lime wedges and cilantro leaves, to garnish

For the sauce

1 tsp grated fresh ginger root
2 tbsp tomato paste
1 tsp sugar
1 tsp salt
1 tbsp chili sauce
1 tbsp malt vinegar
1¼ cups water

1 Rinse, pat dry and place the fish fillets in a medium bowl. Add the lemon juice, fresh cilantro and oil and rub into the fish. Leave to marinate for at least 1 hour. The flavor will improve if you can leave it for longer.

2 To make the sauce, mix together all the sauce ingredients, pour into a small saucepan and simmer over a low heat for about 6 minutes, stirring occasionally.

3 Preheat the broiler to medium. Cook the fillets under the broiler for about 5–7 minutes.

4 When the fillets are cooked, remove and arrange them on a warmed serving dish.

5 The chili sauce should now be fairly thick – about the consistency of a thick chicken soup.

6 Spoon the sauce over the fillets, garnish with the lime wedges and cilantro leaves, and serve with rice.

NUTRITION NOTES

Per portion:
Energy	140Kcals/586kJ
Fat	5.28g
Saturated fat	0.78g
Cholesterol	47.25mg

STEAMING MUSSELS WITH A SPICY SAUCE

──── INGREDIENTS ────

Serves 4
5 tbsp red lentils
2 loaves French bread
4–4½lb live mussels
5 tbsp dry white wine

For the dipping sauce
2 tbsp sunflower oil
1 small onion, finely chopped
½ celery stalk, finely chopped
1 large garlic clove, crushed
1 tsp medium-hot curry paste

1 Soak the lentils in a bowl filled with plenty of cold water until they are required. Preheat the oven to 300°F and put the bread in to warm. Clean the mussels in plenty of cold water and pull off any stray beards. Discard any of the mussels that are damaged or do not close when tapped.

2 Place the mussels in a large saucepan or flameproof casserole. Add the white wine, cover and steam the mussels for about 8 minutes.

3 Transfer the mussels to a colander over a bowl to collect the juices. Keep warm until required.

4 For the dipping sauce, heat the sunflower oil in a second saucepan, add the onion and celery, and cook for about 3–4 minutes to soften without coloring. Strain the mussel juices into a measuring cup to remove any sand or grit. There will be approximately 1⅔ cups of liquid.

COOK'S TIP
Always buy mussels from a reputable supplier and ensure that the shells are tightly closed. Atlantic blue shell mussels are the most common. Small mussels are preferred for their sweet and tender flavor.

5 Add the mussel juices to the saucepan, then add the garlic, curry paste and lentils. Bring to a boil and simmer for a further 10–12 minutes or until the lentils have fallen apart.

6 Tip the mussels out on to four serving plates and serve with the dipping sauce, the warm French bread and a bowl to put the empty shells in.

NUTRITION NOTES	
Per portion:	
Energy	627Kcals/2634kJ
Fat	12.68g
Saturated fat	2.24g
Cholesterol	135mg
Fiber	3.85g

HERRINGS WITH RED SALSA

Herrings are one of the most economical and nutritious fish. If you buy them ready filleted, they're much easier to eat than the whole fish.

INGREDIENTS

Serves 4

2 tbsp skim milk
2 tsp Dijon mustard
2 large herrings, filletted
⅔ cup oatmeal
salt and black pepper

For the salsa

1 small red bell pepper, seeded
4 medium tomatoes
1 scallion, chopped
1 tbsp lime juice
1 tsp granulated sugar

1 Preheat the oven to 400°F. To make the salsa, place the pepper, tomatoes, scallion, lime juice, sugar, and seasoning in a food processor. Process until finely chopped.

2 Mix the milk and mustard, and the oatmeal, and pepper. Dip fillets into the milk mixture, then oatmeal to coat.

3 Place on a baking sheet, then bake for 20 minutes. Serve with the salsa.

NUTRITION NOTES	
Per portion:	
Energy	261Kcals/1097kJ
Fat	15.56g
Saturated fat	3.17g
Cholesterol	52.65mg
Fiber	2.21g

SPICED RAINBOW TROUT

Farmed rainbow trout are very good value and cook very quickly under a broiler or on a barbecue. Herring and mackerel can be cooked in this way too.

INGREDIENTS

Serves 4

4 large rainbow trout fillets (about 5oz each)
1 tbsp ground coriander
1 garlic clove, crushed
2 tbsp finely chopped fresh mint
1 tsp paprika
¾ cup plain yogurt
salad and pita bread, to serve

1 With a sharp knife, slash the flesh of the fish fillets through the skin fairly deeply at intervals.

2 Mix together the coriander, garlic, mint, paprika, and yogurt. Spread this mixture evenly over the fish and leave to marinate for about 1 hour.

3 Cook the fish under a moderately hot broiler or on a barbecue, turning occasionally, until crisp and golden. Serve hot, with a crisp salad and some warmed pita bread.

> COOK'S TIP
> If you are using the broiler, it is best to line the pan with foil before cooking the trout.

NUTRITION NOTES	
Per portion:	
Energy	188Kcals/792kJ
Fat	5.66g
Saturated fat	1.45g
Cholesterol	110.87mg
Fiber	0.05g

FISH BALLS IN TOMATO SAUCE

This quick meal is a good choice for young children, as you can guarantee no bones. If you like, add a dash of chili sauce.

INGREDIENTS

Serves 4

1 lb white fish fillets such as cod or
    flounder, skinned
4 tbsp fresh whole-wheat bread crumbs
2 tbsp snipped chives or scallions
14oz can chopped tomatoes
¾ cup button mushrooms, sliced
salt and black pepper

1 Cut the fish fillets into large chunks and place in a food processor. Add the whole-wheat bread crumbs and chives or scallions. Season to taste with salt and pepper, and process until the fish is finely chopped but still has some texture left.

2 Divide the fish mixture into about 16 even-sized pieces, then shape them into balls with your hands.

3 Place the tomatoes and mushrooms in a wide saucepan and cook over medium heat until boiling. Add the fish balls, cover and simmer for about 10 minutes, until cooked. Serve hot.

COOK'S TIP
The fish balls can be prepared several hours in advance if covered and kept in the refrigerator.

NUTRITION NOTES

Per portion:
Energy	138Kcals/580kJ
Fat	1.38g
Saturated fat	0.24g
Cholesterol	51.75mg
Fiber	1.89g

TUNA AND CORN FISH CAKES

These economical little tuna fish cakes are quick to make. Either use fresh mashed potatoes, or make a less fussy version with instant mashed potatoes.

INGREDIENTS

Serves 4

1¼ cups cooked mashed potatoes
7oz can tuna in vegetable oil, drained
¾ cup canned or frozen corn kernels
2 tbsp chopped fresh parsley
1 cup fresh white or whole-wheat bread crumbs
salt and black pepper
lemon wedges, to serve

1 Place the mashed potato in a bowl and stir in the tuna, corn kernels, and chopped parsley.

2 Season to taste with salt and pepper, then shape into eight patty shapes with your hands.

3 Spread out the bread crumbs on a plate and press the fish cakes into the bread crumbs to coat lightly, then place on a baking sheet.

4 Cook the fish cakes under a moderately hot broiler until crisp and golden brown, turning once. Serve hot, with lemon wedges and fresh vegetables.

COOK'S TIP

For simple variations that are just as pleasing and nutritious, try using canned sardines, red or pink salmon, or smoked mackerel in place of the tuna.

NUTRITION NOTES

Per portion:

Energy	203Kcals/852kJ
Fat	4.62g
Saturated fat	0.81g
Cholesterol	21.25mg
Fiber	1.82g

FISH AND VEGETABLE KEBABS

INGREDIENTS

Serves 4

10oz cod fillets, or any other firm,
  white fish fillets
3 tbsp lemon juice
1 tsp grated fresh ginger root
2 green chilies, very finely chopped
1 tbsp very finely chopped
  fresh cilantro
1 tbsp very finely chopped
  fresh mint
1 tsp ground cilantro
1 tsp salt
1 red bell pepper
1 green bell pepper
½ cauliflower
8 button mushrooms
8 cherry tomatoes
1 tbsp soya oil
1 lime, quartered, to garnish

COOK'S TIP
Use different vegetables to the ones
suggested, if wished. Try baby corn
instead of mushrooms and broccoli
in place of the cauliflower.

1 Cut the fish fillets into large chunks using a sharp knife.

2 In a large mixing bowl, blend together the lemon juice, ginger, chopped green chilies, fresh cilantro, mint, ground cilantro and salt. Add the fish chunks and leave to marinate for about 30 minutes.

3 Cut the red and green bell peppers into large squares and divide the cauliflower into individual florets.

4 Preheat the broiler to hot. Arrange the prepared vegetables alternately with the fish pieces on four skewers.

5 Baste the kebabs with the oil and any remaining marinade. Transfer to a flameproof dish and broil for about 7–10 minutes or until the fish is cooked right through. Garnish with the lime quarters, and serve the kebabs on their own or with saffron rice.

NUTRITION NOTES

Per portion:

Energy	130Kcals/546kJ
Fat	4.34g
Saturated fat	0.51g
Cholesterol	32.54mg

GLAZED GARLIC SHRIMP

A fairly simple and quick dish to prepare, it is best to peel the shrimp as this helps them to absorb maximum flavor. Serve as a main course with a variety of accompaniments, or with a salad as an appetizer.

INGREDIENTS

Serves 4

1 tbsp sunflower oil
3 garlic cloves, roughly chopped
3 tomatoes, chopped
½ tsp salt
1 tsp crushed dried red chilies
1 tsp lemon juice
1 tbsp mango chutney
1 green chili, chopped
15–20 cooked jumbo shrimp, peeled
fresh cilantro leaves and 2 chopped
  scallions, to garnish

NUTRITION NOTES

Per portion:	
Energy	90Kcals/380kJ
Fat	3.83g
Saturated fat	0.54g
Cholesterol	30.37mg

1 Heat the oil in a medium saucepan, and add the chopped garlic.

2 Lower the heat. Add the chopped tomatoes along with the salt, crushed chilies, lemon juice, mango chutney and chopped fresh chili.

3 Finally add the shrimp, turn up the heat and stir-fry quickly until they are heated through.

4 Transfer to a serving dish. Serve immediately garnished with fresh cilantro leaves and chopped scallions.

COD CREOLE

INGREDIENTS

Serves 4

1 lb cod fillets, skinned
1 tbsp lime or lemon juice
2 tsp olive oil
1 medium onion, finely chopped
1 green bell pepper, seeded and sliced
½ tsp cayenne pepper
½ tsp garlic salt
14oz can chopped tomatoes

NUTRITION NOTES

Per portion:

Energy	130Kcals/546kJ
Fat	2.61g
Saturated fat	0.38g
Cholesterol	51.75mg
Fiber	1.61g

1 Cut the cod fillets into bite-sized chunks and sprinkle with the lime or lemon juice.

2 In a large, nonstick pan, heat the olive oil and sauté the onion and pepper gently until softened. Add the cayenne pepper and garlic salt.

3 Stir in the cod with the chopped tomatoes. Bring to a boil, then cover and simmer for about 5 minutes, or until the fish flakes easily. Serve with boiled rice or potatoes.

FIVE-SPICE FISH

Chinese mixtures of spicy, sweet, and sour flavors are particularly successful with fish, and dinner is ready in minutes.

INGREDIENTS

Serves 4

4 white fish fillets, such as cod, haddock or flounder (about 6oz each)
1 tsp Chinese five-spice powder
4 tsp cornstarch
1 tbsp sesame or sunflower oil
3 scallions, shredded
1 tsp finely chopped ginger
5oz button mushrooms, sliced
4oz baby corn, sliced
2 tbsp soy sauce
3 tbsp dry sherry or apple juice
1 tsp sugar
salt and black pepper

1 Toss the fish in the five-spice powder and cornstarch to coat.

2 Heat the oil in a frying pan or wok and stir-fry the scallions, ginger, mushrooms, and corn for about 1 minute. Add the fish and cook for 2–3 minutes, turning once.

3 Mix together the soy sauce, sherry, and sugar, then pour over the fish. Simmer for 2 minutes, adjust the seasoning, then serve with noodles and stir-fried vegetables.

NUTRITION NOTES

Per portion:

Energy	213Kcals/893kJ
Fat	4.41g
Saturated fat	0.67g
Cholesterol	80.5mg
Fiber	1.08g

BROILED SNAPPER WITH MANGO SALSA

INGREDIENTS

Serves 4

12oz new potatoes
3 eggs
4oz green beans, topped, tailed and halved
4 red snapper, about 12oz each, scaled and gutted
2 tbsp olive oil
6oz mixed lettuce leaves
10 cherry tomatoes, to serve
salt and black pepper

For the salsa

3 tbsp chopped fresh cilantro
1 ripe mango, peeled, pitted and diced
½ red chili, seeded and chopped
1in fresh ginger root, grated
juice of 2 limes
generous pinch of celery salt

NUTRITION NOTES

Per portion:

Energy	405Kcals/1702kJ
Fat	15.59g
Saturated fat	2.06g
Cholesterol	163.62mg
Fiber	2.03g

1 Place the potatoes in a large saucepan and cover with cold salted water. Bring to a boil and simmer for about 15–20 minutes until tender. Drain and set aside.

2 Bring a second large pan of salted water to a boil. Put in the eggs and boil for 4 minutes.

3 Add the beans and cook for about 6 minutes more, so that the eggs have a total of 10 minutes. Remove the eggs from the pan, cool, peel and cut into quarters. Drain the beans and set aside.

4 Preheat a moderate broiler. Slash each snapper three times on either side, moisten with oil and cook for about 12 minutes, turning once.

5 For the dressing, place the cilantro in a food processor or blender. Add the mango, chili, ginger, lime juice and celery salt, and process until smooth.

6 Moisten the lettuce leaves with olive oil, and divide them among four large plates.

7 Arrange the snapper over the lettuce and season to taste. Halve the new potatoes and tomatoes, and distribute them with the beans and quartered hard-boiled eggs over the salad. Serve with the salsa dressing.

SALMON RISOTTO WITH CUCUMBER

Any rice can be used for risotto, although the creamiest ones are made with short grain arborio and carnaroli rice. Fresh tarragon and cucumber combine well to bring out the flavor of the salmon.

INGREDIENTS

Serves 4

2 tbsp sunflower margarine
1 small bunch scallions, white part only, chopped
½ cucumber, peeled, seeded and chopped
1¾ cups short grain risotto rice
3¾ cups chicken or fish broth
⅔ cup dry white wine
1lb salmon fillet, skinned and diced
3 tbsp chopped fresh tarragon

COOK'S TIP
Long grain rice can be used for this recipe in place of the short grain risotto rice. If using long grain rice, reduce the broth to 3²/₃ cups.

1 Heat the margarine in a large saucepan, and add the scallions and cucumber. Cook for about 2–3 minutes without coloring.

2 Add the rice, broth and wine and return to a boil.

3 Simmer the wine and broth mixture for about 10 minutes, stirring occasionally. Stir in the diced salmon and tarragon. Continue cooking for 5 minutes more, then switch off the heat. Cover and leave to stand for 5 minutes before serving.

NUTRITION NOTES

Per portion:

Energy	653Kcals/2742kJ
Fat	19.88g
Saturated fat	6.99g
Cholesterol	70.63mg
Fiber	0.91g

JAMAICAN COD STEAKS WITH RAGOÛT

Spicy hot from Kingston town, this is a fast fish dish.

— INGREDIENTS —

Serves 4

finely grated zest of ½ orange
2 tbsp black peppercorns
1 tbsp allspice berries or Jamaican pepper
½ tsp salt
4 cod fillet steaks, about 6oz each
peanut oil, for frying
new potatoes, to serve (optional)
3 tbsp chopped fresh parsley, to garnish

For the ragout

2 tbsp peanut oil
1 onion, chopped
1in piece fresh ginger root, peeled and grated
1lb fresh pumpkin, peeled, seeded and chopped
3–4 shakes of Tabasco sauce
2 tbsp soft brown sugar
1 tbsp vinegar

1 For the ragout, heat the oil in a heavy saucepan and add the onion and ginger. Cover and cook, stirring, for 3–4 minutes until soft.

2 Add the chopped pumpkin, Tabasco sauce, brown sugar and vinegar, cover and cook over a low heat for about 10–12 minutes until softened.

3 Combine the orange zest, peppercorns, allspice or Jamaican pepper and salt, then crush coarsely using a pestle and mortar. (Alternatively, coarsely grind the peppercorns in a pepper mill and combine with the zest and seasoning.)

4 Sprinkle the spice mixture over both sides of the fish and moisten with a little oil.

5 Heat a large frying pan, add the cod steaks and dry-fry for about 12 minutes, turning once.

6 Serve the cod steaks with a spoonful of pumpkin ragout and new potatoes, if required, and garnish the ragout with chopped fresh parsley.

— NUTRITION NOTES —

Per portion:

Energy	324Kcals/1360kJ
Fat	14.9g
Saturated fat	2.75g
Cholesterol	80.5mg
Fiber	1.92g

COOK'S TIP

This recipe can be adapted using any type of firm pink or white fish that is available, such as haddock, whiting, monkfish, halibut or tuna.

TUNA AND FLAGEOLET BEAN SALAD

Two cans of tuna fish form the basis of this delicious and easy-to-make storecupboard salad.

INGREDIENTS

Serves 4

6 tbsp reduced calorie mayonnaise
1 tsp mustard
2 tbsp capers
3 tbsp chopped fresh parsley
pinch of celery salt
2 x 7oz cans tuna in brine,
  drained
3 Bibb lettuces
14oz can flageolet beans, drained
12 cherry tomatoes, halved
14oz can baby artichoke hearts,
  halved
toasted sesame bread or sticks,
  to serve

NUTRITION NOTES

Per portion:	
Energy	299Kcals/1255kJ
Fat	13.91g
Saturated fat	2.12g
Cholesterol	33mg
Fiber	6.36g

1 Combine the mayonnaise, mustard, capers and parsley in a mixing bowl. Season to taste with celery salt.

2 Flake the tuna into the dressing and toss gently.

3 Arrange the lettuce leaves on four plates, then spoon the tuna mixture on to the leaves.

COOK'S TIP
If flageolet beans are not available, use cannellini beans.

4 Spoon the flageolet beans to one side, followed by the tomatoes and artichoke hearts.

5 Serve with slices of toasted sesame bread or sticks.

PASTA, PIZZAS, PULSES AND GRAINS

Pasta, pizzas, pulses and grain dishes should be encouraged at family meals as they're mostly very healthy foods. Pasta and rice contain good amounts of protein, carbohydrate and vitamins, are particularly low in fat, and are also extremely versatile.

Add variety to meals by introducing different grains, such as polenta, couscous or bulgur wheat, which are just as easy and healthy as rice, but will help to keep appetites lively.

PENNE AND EGGPLANT WITH MINT PESTO

This splendid variation on the classic Italian pesto uses fresh mint rather than basil.

INGREDIENTS

Serves 4
2 large eggplants
pinch of salt
5 cups penne
½ cup walnut halves

For the pesto
1 cup fresh mint
½ cup flat leaf parsley
½ cup walnuts
½ cup Parmesan cheese, finely
  grated
2 garlic cloves
3 tbsp olive oil
salt and black pepper

NUTRITION NOTES

Per portion:
Energy	777Kcals/2364kJ
Fat	38.11g
Saturated fat	6.29g
Cholesterol	10mg
Fiber	8.57g

1 Cut the eggplants lengthwise into ½in slices.

2 Cut the slices again crossways to give short strips.

3 Layer the strips in a colander with salt and leave to stand for 30 minutes over a plate to catch any juices. Rinse well in cool water and drain.

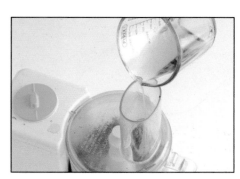

4 For the pesto, place all the ingredients, except the oil, in a food processor or blender and process until smooth, then gradually add the oil in a thin stream until the mixture comes together. Season to taste.

5 Bring a large saucepan of water to a boil, toss in the penne and cook for 8 minutes or until nearly cooked. Add the eggplant and cook for 3 minutes more.

6 Drain well and mix in half of the mint pesto and walnut halves. Serve with the remaining pesto and walnut halves on top.

TAGLIATELLE WITH PEA AND BEAN SAUCE

A creamy pea sauce makes a wonderful combination with the crunchy young vegetables.

INGREDIENTS

Serves 4

1 tbsp olive oil

1 garlic clove, crushed

6 scallions, sliced

1 cup fresh or frozen baby peas, defrosted

12oz fresh young asparagus

2 tbsp chopped fresh sage, plus extra leaves, to garnish

finely grated rind of 2 lemons

1²/₃ cups vegetable broth or water

1½ cups fresh or frozen fava beans, defrosted

1lb tagliatelle

4 tbsp plain low fat yogurt

NUTRITION NOTES

Per portion:

Energy	509 Kcals/2139kJ
Fat	6.75g
Saturated fat	0.95g
Cholesterol	0.6mg
Fiber	9.75g

1 Heat the oil in a pan. Add the garlic and scallions, and cook gently for about 2–3 minutes until softened.

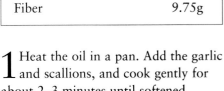

2 Add the peas and a third of the asparagus, together with the sage, lemon rind and broth or water. Simmer for about 10 minutes. Process in a food processor or blender until smooth.

3 Meanwhile remove the outer skins from the fava beans and discard.

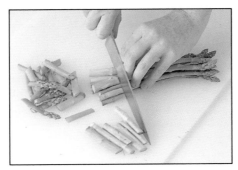

4 Cut the remaining asparagus into 2in lengths, trimming off any tough fibrous stems, and blanch in boiling water for about 2 minutes.

5 Cook the tagliatelle following the manufacturer's instructions until *al dente*. Drain well.

6 Add the cooked asparagus and shelled beans to the sauce, and reheat. Stir in the yogurt and toss into the tagliatelle. Garnish with a few extra sage leaves, and serve immediately.

COOK'S TIP
Frozen peas and beans have been suggested as an option here to cut down the preparation time, but the dish tastes even better if you use fresh young vegetables when in season.

SPAGHETTI WITH HERB SAUCE

INGREDIENTS

Serves 4

*2 cups chopped fresh mixed herbs, such
as parsley, basil and thyme*
2 garlic cloves, crushed
4 tbsp pine nuts, toasted
4 tbsp olive oil
12oz dried spaghetti
4 tbsp grated Parmesan cheese
salt and black pepper
basil leaves, to garnish

COOK'S TIP

Spaghetti should be cooked until
it is just firm to the bite, or *al
dente*. If it is allowed to cook for
too long, it will become soggy.

---

1 Put the herbs, garlic and half the
pine nuts into a food processor or
blender. With the machine running,
gradually add the oil and process to
form a thick paste.

2 Cook the spaghetti in plenty of
boiling salted water for about
8 minutes until *al dente*. Drain.

NUTRITION NOTES

Per portion:

Energy	694Kcals/2915kJ
Fat	42.01g
Saturated fat	6.80g
Cholesterol	7.50mg
Fiber	3.18g

3 Transfer the herb paste to a large
warm bowl, then add the spaghetti
and Parmesan. Toss well to coat the
pasta with the sauce. Sprinkle over the
remaining pine nuts and the basil
leaves, and serve immediately.

CHIVE OMELETTE STIR-FRY

INGREDIENTS

Serves 3–4

2 eggs
1–2 tbsp snipped fresh chives
2 tbsp peanut oil
1 garlic clove, chopped
*½in piece fresh ginger root,
chopped*
2 celery stalks, cut into shreds
2 carrots, cut into shreds
2 small zucchini, cut into shreds
4 scallions, cut into shreds
1 bunch radishes, sliced
1⅓ cup beansprouts
¼ head of Chinese leaves, shredded
1 tbsp sesame oil
salt and black pepper

NUTRITION NOTES

Per portion:

Energy	188Kcals/788kJ
Fat	13.3g
Saturated fat	2.76g
Cholesterol	146.3mg
Fiber	3.85g

---

1 Whisk together the eggs, chives and
seasoning in a bowl. Heat about
1 tsp of the peanut oil in an omelette
pan and pour in just enough of the egg
mixture to cover the base of the pan.
Cook for about 1 minute until set, then
turn over the omelette and cook for
1 minute more.

2 Tip out the omelette on to a plate
and cook the rest of the egg mixture
in the same way to make several
omelettes, adding extra oil to the pan,
if neccessary. Roll up each omelette and
slice thinly. Keep the omelettes warm in
a low oven until required.

3 Heat the remaining oil in a wok or
large frying pan, add the chopped
garlic and ginger and stir-fry for a few
seconds to flavor the oil.

4 Add the shredded celery, carrots
and zucchini, and stir-fry the
vegetables for about 1 minute. Add the
radishes, beansprouts, scallions and
Chinese leaves and stir-fry for 2–3
minutes more, until all the vegetables
are tender but still crunchy. Sprinkle a
little sesame oil over the vegetables and
toss gently.

5 Serve the stir-fried vegetables at
once with the sliced chive omelettes
scattered over the top.

TABBOULEH WITH FENNEL

A fresh salad originating in the Middle East that is perfect for a summer lunch. Serve with lettuce and pita bread.

INGREDIENTS

Serves 4
1¼ cups bulgur wheat
2 fennel bulbs
1 small red chili, seeded and chopped
1 celery stalk, finely sliced
2 tbsp olive oil
finely grated rind and juice of
    2 lemons
6–8 scallions, chopped
6 tbsp chopped fresh mint
6 tbsp chopped fresh parsley
1 pomegranate, seeded
salt and black pepper

NUTRITION NOTES

Per portion:
Energy   188Kcals/791kJ
Fat   4.67g
Saturated fat   0.62g
Cholesterol   0
Fiber   2.17g

1 Place the bulgur wheat in a bowl and pour over enough cold water to cover. Leave to stand for 30 minutes.

3 Halve the fennel bulbs and carefully cut them into very fine slices with a sharp knife.

2 Drain the wheat through a strainer, pressing out any excess water using a spoon.

4 Mix all the remaining ingredients together, including the soaked bulgur wheat and fennel. Season well, cover, and set aside for 30 minutes before serving.

COOK'S TIP
Fennel has a very distinctive aniseed flavor. When you are buying fennel, choose well-rounded bulbs which are pale green to white in color. Avoid any that are deep green. Fennel never goes out of season – it is available all year round.

SWEET VEGETABLE COUSCOUS

A wonderful combination of sweet vegetables and spices, this makes a substantial winter dish.

INGREDIENTS

Serves 4–6
generous pinch of saffron threads
3 tbsp boiling water
1 tbsp olive oil
1 red onion, sliced
2 garlic cloves
1–2 red chilies, seeded and finely chopped
½ tsp ground ginger
½ tsp ground cinnamon
14oz can chopped tomatoes
1¼ cups fresh vegetable broth or water
4 carrots, peeled and cut into ¼in slices
2 turnips, peeled and cut into ¾in cubes
1lb sweet potatoes, peeled and cut into ¾in cubes
⅔ cup raisins
2 zucchini, cut into ¼in slices
14oz can chick-peas, drained and rinsed
3 tbsp chopped fresh parsley
3 tbsp chopped fresh cilantro
4 cups quick-cook couscous

1 Leave the saffron to infuse in the boiling water.

2 Heat the oil in a large saucepan or flameproof casserole. Add the onion, garlic and chilies, and cook gently for about 5 minutes.

3 Add the ginger and cinnamon to the pan or casserole, and cook gently for 1–2 minutes more.

4 Add the tomatoes, broth or water, saffron and liquid, carrots, turnips, sweet potatoes and raisins, cover and simmer for 25 minutes more.

5 Add the zucchini, chick-peas, parsley and cilantro, and cook for 10 minutes more.

6 Meanwhile prepare the couscous following the manufacturer's instructions, and then serve with the prepared vegetables.

NUTRITION NOTES

Per portion:

Energy	570Kcals/2393kJ
Fat	7.02g
Saturated fat	0.83g
Cholesterol	0
Fiber	10.04g

COOK'S TIP
Vegetable broth can be made from a variety of uncooked vegetables. These can include the outer leaves of cabbage, lettuce and other greens, carrot peelings, leeks as well as parsnips.

Pasta with Chick Pea Sauce

Serves 4
2 cups pasta
1 tsp olive oil
1 small onion, finely chopped
1 garlic clove, crushed
1 celery stalk, finely chopped
15oz can chick peas, drained
1 cup tomato sauce
salt and black pepper
chopped fresh parsley, to garnish

1 Heat the olive oil in a nonstick pan and sauté the onion, garlic, and celery until softened, not browned. Stir in the chick peas and tomato sauce, then cover and simmer for about 15 minutes.

2 Cook the pasta in a large pan of boiling, lightly salted water until just tender. Drain the pasta and toss into the sauce, then season to taste with salt and pepper. Sprinkle with chopped fresh parsley, then serve hot.

Nutrition Notes

Per portion:

Energy	374Kcals/1570kJ
Fat	4.44g
Saturated fat	0.32g
Cholesterol	0
Fiber	6.41g

Peperonata Pizza

Makes 2 large pizzas
4 cups flour
pinch of salt
1 envelope active dry yeast
about 1½ cups warm water

For the topping
1 onion, sliced
2 tsp olive oil
2 large red and 2 yellow bell peppers, seeded and sliced
1 garlic clove, crushed
14oz can tomatoes
8 pitted ripe olives, halved
salt and black pepper

1 To make the dough, sift the flour and salt into a bowl and stir in the yeast. Stir in just enough warm water to mix to a soft dough.

2 Knead for 5 minutes until smooth. Cover and leave in a warm place for about 1 hour, or until doubled in size.

3 To make the topping, sauté the onion in the oil until soft, then stir in the peppers, garlic, and tomatoes. Cover and simmer for 30 minutes, until no liquid remains. Season to taste.

4 Preheat the oven to 450°F. Divide the dough in half and press out each piece on a lightly oiled baking sheet to a 11in round, turning up the edges slightly.

5 Spread over the topping, dot with olives, and bake for 15–20 minutes. Serve hot or cold, with salad.

Nutrition Notes

Per portion:

Energy	965Kcals/4052kJ
Fat	9.04g
Saturated fat	1.07g
Cholesterol	0
Fiber	14.51g

CAMPANELLE WITH BELL PEPPER SAUCE

Roasted yellow bell peppers make a deliciously sweet and creamy sauce for pasta.

INGREDIENTS

Serves 4
2 yellow bell peppers, halved
¼ cup low fat soft goat cheese
½ cup low fat ricotta cheese
salt and black pepper
5 cups campanelle pasta
¼ cup sliced almonds, toasted,
   to serve

NUTRITION NOTES

Per portion:
Energy	529Kcals/2221kJ
Fat	11.18 g
Saturated fat	0.88g
Cholesterol	9.04mg
Fiber	5.69g

1 Preheat the broiler. Place the bell pepper halves under the broiler until charred and blistered. Place in a plastic bag to cool. Peel and remove the seeds.

> **COOK'S TIP**
> Always cut the stalk ends from bell peppers and discard the mid-ribs and seeds.

2 Place the bell pepper flesh in a food processor or blender with the goat cheese and ricotta cheese. Process until smooth. Season with salt and lots of black pepper.

3 Cook the pasta following the manufacturer's instructions until *al dente*. Drain well.

4 Toss with the sauce and serve the dish sprinkled with the toasted sliced almonds.

Green Lentil and Cabbage Salad

This warm crunchy salad makes a satisfying meal if served with crusty French bread or whole-wheat rolls.

Ingredients

Serves 4–6

1¼ cups green lentils
6 cups cold water
1 garlic clove
1 bay leaf
1 small onion, peeled and studded with
  2 cloves
1 tbsp olive oil
1 red onion, finely sliced
2 garlic cloves, crushed
1 tbsp thyme leaves
3¾ cups cabbage, finely shredded
finely grated rind and juice of 1 lemon
1 tbsp raspberry vinegar
salt and black pepper

Nutrition Notes

Per portion:

Energy	228Kcals/959kJ
Fat	4.38g
Saturated fat	0.44g
Cholesterol	0
Fiber	8.09g

1 Rinse the lentils in cold water and place in a large pan with the water, peeled garlic clove, bay leaf and clove-studded onion. Bring to a boil and cook for about 10 minutes. Reduce the heat, cover the pan, and simmer gently for 15–20 minutes more. Drain and remove the onion, garlic and bay leaf.

2 Heat the oil in a large pan. Add the red onion, garlic and thyme, and cook for 5 minutes until softened.

3 Add the cabbage and cook for 3–5 minutes more until just cooked but still crunchy (*al dente*).

4 Stir in the cooked lentils, lemon rind and juice and the raspberry vinegar. Season to taste and serve.

Cook's Tip

There are several varieties of cabbage such as spring, summer, winter, white and red cabbage. White cabbage is excellent in salads; choose one with a firm, compact head and avoid those that have loose curling leaves.

Lemon and Ginger Spicy Beans

Ingredients

Serves 4

*2 tbsp roughly chopped fresh
 ginger root*
3 garlic cloves, roughly chopped
1 cup cold water
1 tbsp sunflower oil
1 large onion, thinly sliced
*1 red chili, seeded and finely
 chopped*
¼ tsp cayenne pepper
2 tsp ground cumin
1 tsp ground cilantro
½ tsp ground turmeric
2 tbsp lemon juice
3 cups chopped fresh cilantro
*14oz can black-eyed beans, drained
 and rinsed*
*14oz can aduki beans, drained
 and rinsed*
*14oz can navy beans, drained
 and rinsed*
salt and black pepper
crusty bread, to serve

1 Place the ginger, garlic and 4 tbsp of
the cold water in a food processor
or blender and process for 1–2 minutes
until smooth.

2 Heat the oil in a saucepan. Add the
onion and chili, and cook gently for
about 5 minutes until softened.

3 Add the cayenne pepper, cumin,
ground cilantro and turmeric, and
stir-fry for 1 minute more.

4 Stir in the ginger and garlic paste
from the food processor or blender
and cook for 1 minute more.

5 Add the remaining water, lemon
juice and fresh cilantro, stir well
and bring to a boil. Cover the pan
tightly and cook for about 5 minutes.

6 Add all the beans and cook for
5–10 minutes more. Season with
salt and pepper, to taste, and serve with
crusty bread.

Nutrition Notes	
Per portion:	
Energy	281Kcals/1180kJ
Fat	4.3g
Saturated fat	0.42g
Cholesterol	0
Fiber	10.76g

SESAME NOODLE SALAD WITH PEANUTS

An Orient-inspired salad with crunchy vegetables and a light soy dressing. The hot peanuts make a surprisingly successful union with the cold noodles.

INGREDIENTS

Serves 4

12oz egg noodles
2 carrots, peeled and cut into fine
    julienne strips
½ cucumber, peeled and cut into
    ½in cubes
4oz celeriac, peeled and cut into fine
    julienne strips
6 scallions, finely sliced
8 canned water chestnuts, drained and
    finely sliced
2 cups beansprouts
1 small green chili, chopped, plus
    1 green chili, to garnish
2 tbsp sesame seeds and 1 cup peanuts,
    to serve

For the dressing

1 tbsp dark soy sauce
1 tbsp light soy sauce
1 tbsp clear honey
1 tbsp rice wine or dry sherry
1 tbsp sesame oil

1 Preheat the oven to 400°F. Bring a large saucepan of water to a boil, toss in the egg noodles and cook according to the manufacturer's instructions.

2 Drain the noodles, refresh in cold water, then drain again.

3 Mix the noodles with all of the prepared vegetables.

4 For the dressing, combine the ingredients in a bowl, then toss into the vegetable mixture. Divide the salad among four plates.

5 Place the sesame seeds and peanuts on separate cookie sheets and bake for 5 minutes. Remove the sesame seeds and continue to cook the peanuts for 5 minutes more, or until browned.

6 Sprinkle the sesame seeds and peanuts over each portion and serve at once, garnished with chilies.

NUTRITION NOTES	
Per portion:	
Energy	634Kcals/2664kJ
Fat	28.1g
Saturated fat	4.03g
Cholesterol	0
Fiber	5.33g

PENNE WITH BROCCOLI AND CHILI

Serves 4

1 lb small broccoli florets
2 tbsp broth
1 garlic clove, crushed
1 small red chili pepper, sliced, or ½ tsp
  chili sauce
4 tbsp plain low fat yogurt
2 tbsp toasted pine nuts or cashews
3¼ cups penne pasta
salt and black pepper

2 Heat the broth and add the crushed garlic and chili or chili sauce. Stir over low heat for 2–3 minutes.

1 Add the pasta to a large pan of lightly salted boiling water and return to a boil. Place the broccoli in a steamer basket over the top. Cover and cook for 8–10 minutes until both are just tender. Drain.

3 Stir in the broccoli, pasta, and yogurt. Adjust the seasoning, sprinkle with nuts, and serve hot.

NUTRITION NOTES

Per portion:
Energy   403Kcals/1695kJ
Fat   7.87g
Saturated fat   0.89g
Cholesterol   0.6mg
Fiber   5.83g

CREOLE JAMBALAYA

Serves 6

4 boneless chicken thighs, skinned and
  diced
1 large green bell pepper, seeded and
  sliced
3 celery stalks, sliced
4 scallions, sliced
about 1¼ cups chicken broth
14oz can tomatoes
1 tsp ground cumin
1 tsp ground allspice
½ tsp cayenne pepper
1 tsp dried thyme
1½ cups long-grain rice
7oz cooked, peeled shrimp
salt and black pepper

2 Add the pepper, celery, and onions with 1 tbsp broth. Cook for a few minutes to soften, then add the tomatoes, spices, and thyme.

1 Brown the chicken in a nonstick pan without fat, turning occasionally, until golden all over.

3 Stir in the rice and broth. Cover and cook for about 20 minutes, stirring occasionally, until the rice is tender. Add more broth if necessary.

4 Add the shrimp and heat well. Season and serve with a crisp salad.

NUTRITION NOTES

Per portion:
Energy   282Kcals/1185kJ
Fat   3.37g
Saturated fat   0.85g
Cholesterol   51.33mg
Fiber   1.55g

THAI FRAGRANT RICE

A lovely, soft, fluffy rice dish, perfumed with delicious and fresh lemon grass.

INGREDIENTS

Serves 4

1 piece lemon grass
2 limes
1⅓ cups brown basmati rice
1 tbsp olive oil
1 onion, chopped
1in piece fresh ginger root, peeled and finely chopped
1½ tsp cilantro seeds
1½ tsp cumin seeds
3⅔ cups vegetable broth
4 tbsp chopped fresh cilantro
lime wedges, to serve

COOK'S TIP
Other varieties of rice, such as white basmati or long grain, can be used for this dish but you will need to adjust the cooking times as necessary.

1 Finely chop the lemon grass and remove the zest from the limes.

2 Rinse the rice in cold water. Drain through a strainer.

3 Heat the oil in a large saucepan and add the onion and spices and cook gently for about 2–3 minutes.

4 Add the rice and cook for 1 minute more, then add the broth or water and bring to the boil. Reduce the heat to very low and cover the pan. Cook gently for about 30 minutes then check the rice. If it is still crunchy, cover the pan again with the lid and leave for 3–5 minutes more. Remove the pan from the heat.

5 Stir in the fresh cilantro, fluff up the grains, cover and keep warm for 10 minutes. Serve with lime wedges.

NUTRITION NOTES

Per portion:

Energy	259Kcals/1087kJ
Fat	5.27g
Saturated fat	0.81g
Cholesterol	0
Fiber	1.49g

PUMPKIN AND PISTACHIO RISOTTO

This elegant combination of creamy golden rice and orange pumpkin can be made as pale or bright as you like – simply add different quantities of saffron.

─ INGREDIENTS ─

Serves 4

5 cups vegetable broth or water
generous pinch of saffron threads
2 tbsp olive oil
1 onion, chopped
2 garlic cloves, crushed
2lb pumpkin, peeled, seeded and cut
into ¾in cubes
2 cups arborio rice
⅞ cup dry white wine
1 tbsp finely grated Parmesan cheese
½ cup pistachios
3 tbsp chopped fresh marjoram or
oregano, plus a few extra leaves,
to garnish
salt, freshly grated nutmeg and black
pepper

─ NUTRITION NOTES ─

Per portion:

Energy	630Kcals/2646kJ
Fat	15.24g
Saturated fat	2.66g
Cholesterol	3.75mg
Fiber	2.59g

1 Bring the broth or water to a boil and reduce to a low simmer. Ladle a little liquid into a small bowl. Add the saffron threads and leave to infuse.

2 Heat the oil in a saucepan or flameproof casserole. Add the onion and garlic, and cook for 5 minutes until softened. Add the pumpkin and rice and cook for a few minutes more until the rice looks transparent.

3 Pour in the wine and allow it to boil hard. When it is absorbed add a quarter of the broth or water and the infused saffron and liquid. Stir until all the liquid is absorbed.

4 Gradually add a ladleful of broth or water at a time, allowing the rice to absorb the liquid before adding more and stir constantly.

5 Cook the rice for about 25–30 minutes or until *al dente*. Stir in the Parmesan cheese, cover the pan and leave to stand for 5 minutes.

6 To finish, stir in the pistachios and marjoram or oregano. Season to taste with a little salt, nutmeg and pepper, and sprinkle over a few extra marjoram or oregano leaves.

COOK'S TIP
Italian arborio rice is a special short grain rice that gives an authentic creamy consistency.

TOMATO RICE

This dish is delicious and is substantial enough to be eaten as a complete meal on its own.

INGREDIENTS

Serves 4

2 tbsp corn oil
½ tsp onion seeds
1 onion, sliced
2 tomatoes, sliced
1 orange or yellow bell pepper, chopped
1 tsp grated fresh ginger root
1 garlic clove, crushed
1 tsp chili powder
2 tbsp chopped fresh cilantro
1 potato, diced
1½ tsp salt
½ cup frozen peas
2 cups basmati rice, washed
3 cups water

NUTRITION NOTES

Per portion:

Energy	351Kcals/1475kJ
Fat	6.48g
Saturated fat	0.86g
Cholesterol	0

1 Heat the oil and fry the onion seeds for about 30 seconds. Add the sliced onion and fry for about 5 minutes.

2 Add the next nine ingredients and stir-fry over a medium heat for about 5 minutes more.

3 Add the rice and stir-fry for about 1 minute.

4 Pour in the water and bring to a boil, then lower the heat to medium. Cover and cook for 12–15 minutes more. Leave the rice to stand for 5 minutes and serve.

PEA AND MUSHROOM PULLAO

It is best to use button mushrooms and petit pois for this delectable rice dish, as they make the pullao look very attractive and appetizing.

INGREDIENTS

Serves 6

2¼ cups basmati rice
2 tbsp vegetable oil
½ tsp black cumin seeds
2 black cardamom pods
2 cinnamon sticks
3 garlic cloves, sliced
1 tsp salt
1 tomato, sliced
⅔ cup button mushrooms
⅓ heaped cup petit pois
3⅔ cups water

1 Wash the rice at least twice and set aside in a strainer.

NUTRITION NOTES

Per portion:

Energy	297Kcals/1246kJ
Fat	4.34g
Saturated fat	0.49g
Cholesterol	0

2 Heat the oil in a medium saucepan and add the spices, garlic and salt.

3 Add the sliced tomato and button mushrooms, and stir-fry for about 2–3 minutes.

4 Add the rice and peas, and gently stir around making sure you do not break the rice.

5 Add the water and bring the mixture to a boil. Lower the heat, cover the pan, and continue to cook for 15–20 minutes.

SPINACH AND HAZELNUT LASAGNE

A vegetarian dish that is hearty enough to satisfy meat-eaters too. Use frozen spinach if you're short of time.

INGREDIENTS

Serves 4

2 lb fresh spinach
1¼ cups vegetable or chicken broth
1 medium onion, finely chopped
1 garlic clove, crushed
¾ cup hazelnuts
2 tbsp chopped fresh basil
6 sheets lasagne
14oz can chopped tomatoes
1 cup low fat fromage frais
slivered hazlenuts and chopped parsley,
   to garnish

1 Preheat the oven to 400°F. Wash the spinach and place in a pan with just the water that clings to the leaves. Cook the spinach over a fairly high heat for 2 minutes until wilted. Drain well.

2 Heat 2 tbsp of the broth in a large pan and simmer the onion and garlic until soft. Stir in the spinach, hazelnuts, and basil.

3 In a large ovenproof dish, layer the spinach, lasagne, and tomatoes. Season well between the layers. Pour over the remaining broth. Spread the fromage frais over the top.

4 Bake the lasagne for about 45 minutes, or until golden brown. Serve hot, sprinkled with lines of slivered hazelnuts and chopped parsley.

COOK'S TIP
The flavor of hazelnuts is improved by roasting. Place them on a baking sheet and bake in a moderate oven, or under a hot broiler, until light golden.

NUTRITION NOTES

Per portion:

Energy	365Kcals/1532kJ
Fat	17g
Saturated fat	1.46g
Cholesterol	0.5mg
Fiber	8.16g

CALZONE

Makes 4
4 cups flour
pinch of salt
1 envelope active dry yeast
about 1½ cups warm water

For the filling
1 tsp olive oil
1 medium red onion, thinly sliced
3 medium zucchini, about 12oz total
*   weight, sliced*
2 large tomatoes, diced
1 cup mozzarella cheese, diced
1 tbsp chopped fresh oregano
skim milk, to glaze
salt and black pepper

1 To make the dough, sift the flour and salt into a bowl and stir in the yeast. Stir in just enough warm water to mix to a soft dough.

2 Knead for 5 minutes until smooth. Cover and leave in a warm place for about 1 hour, or until doubled in size.

3 Meanwhile, to make the filling, heat the oil and sauté the onion and zucchini for 3–4 minutes. Remove from the heat and add the tomatoes, cheese, oregano, and seasoning.

4 Preheat the oven to 425°F. Knead the dough lightly and divide into four. Roll out each piece on a lightly floured surface to a 8in round, and place a quarter of the filling on one half.

5 Brush the edges with milk and fold over to enclose the filling. Press firmly to enclose. Brush with milk.

6 Bake on an oiled baking sheet for 15–20 minutes. Serve hot or cold.

NUTRITION NOTES	
Per portion:	
Energy	544Kcals/2285kJ
Fat	10.93g
Saturated fat	5.49g
Cholesterol	24.42mg
Fiber	5.09g

TAGLIATELLE WITH HAZELNUT PESTO

Hazelnuts are lower in fat than other nuts, which makes them useful for this reduced-fat alternative to pesto sauce.

INGREDIENTS

Serves 4

2 garlic cloves, crushed
1 cup fresh basil leaves
¼ cup hazelnuts
⅞ cup skim milk soft cheese
8oz dried tagliatelle, or 1 lb fresh
salt and black pepper

1 Place the garlic, basil, hazelnuts, and cheese in a food processor or blender and process to a thick paste.

2 Cook the tagliatelle in lightly salted boiling water until just tender, then drain well.

3 Spoon the sauce into the hot pasta, tossing until melted. Sprinkle with pepper and serve hot.

NUTRITION NOTES

Per portion:

Energy	274Kcals/1155kJ
Fat	5.05g
Saturated fat	0.43g
Cholesterol	0.5mg
Fiber	2.14g

SPAGHETTI WITH TUNA SAUCE

A speedy mid-week meal, which can also be made with other pasta shapes.

INGREDIENTS

Serves 4

8oz dried spaghetti, or 1 lb fresh
1 garlic clove, crushed
14oz can chopped tomatoes
15oz can tuna in water, flaked
½ tsp chili sauce (optional)
4 pitted ripe olives, chopped
salt and black pepper

COOK'S TIP

If fresh tuna is available, use 1lb, cut into small chunks, and add after step 2. Simmer for 6–8 minutes, then add the chili sauce, olives, and pasta.

1 Cook the spaghetti in lightly salted boiling water for 12 minutes or until just tender. Drain well and keep hot.

2 Add the garlic and tomatoes to the saucepan and bring to a boil. Simmer, uncovered, for 2–3 minutes.

3 Add the tuna, chili sauce, if using, olives, and spaghetti. Heat well, add the seasoning, and serve hot.

NUTRITION NOTES

Per portion:

Energy	306Kcals/1288kJ
Fat	2.02g
Saturated fat	0.37g
Cholesterol	48.45mg
Fiber	2.46g

Bulgur and Lentil Pilaf

Bulgur wheat is very easy to cook and can be used in almost any way you would normally use rice, hot or cold. Some of the finer grades need hardly any cooking, so check the package for cooking times.

— Ingredients —

Serves 4

1 tsp olive oil
1 large onion, thinly sliced
2 garlic cloves, crushed
1 tsp ground coriander
1 tsp ground cumin
1 tsp ground turmeric
½ tsp ground allspice
1¼ cups bulgur wheat
about 3⅔ cups broth or water
1½ cups button mushrooms, sliced
⅔ cup green lentils
salt, black pepper and cayenne

1 Heat the oil in a nonstick saucepan and sauté the onion, garlic, and spices for 1 minute, stirring.

2 Stir in the bulgur wheat and cook, stirring, for about 2 minutes, until lightly browned. Add the broth or water, mushrooms, and lentils.

3 Simmer over very low heat for about 25–30 minutes, until the bulgur wheat and lentils are tender and all the liquid is absorbed. Add more broth or water, if necessary.

4 Season well with salt, pepper, and cayenne and serve hot.

Cook's Tip
Green lentils can be cooked without presoaking, as they cook quite quickly and keep their shape. However, if you have the time, soaking them first will shorten the cooking time slightly.

— Nutrition Notes —

Per portion:

Energy	325Kcals/1367kJ
Fat	2.8g
Saturated fat	0.33g
Cholesterol	0
Fiber	3.61g

MINTED COUSCOUS CASTLES

Couscous is a fine semolina flour made from wheat grain, which is usually steamed and served plain with a rich meat or vegetable stew. Here it is flavored with mint and molded to make an unusual accompaniment to serve with any savory dish.

INGREDIENTS

Serves 6

1¼ cups couscous
2 cups boiling broth
1 tbsp lemon juice
2 tomatoes, diced
2 tbsp chopped fresh mint
oil, for brushing
salt and black pepper
mint sprigs, to garnish

1 Place the couscous in a bowl and pour over the boiling broth. Cover the bowl and leave to stand for 30 minutes, until all the broth is absorbed and the grains are tender.

2 Stir in the lemon juice with the tomatoes and chopped mint. Adjust the seasoning with salt and pepper.

3 Brush the insides of four cups or individual molds with oil. Spoon in the couscous mixture and pack down firmly. Chill for several hours.

4 Turn out and serve cold, or alternatively, cover and heat gently in a low oven or microwave, then turn out and serve hot, garnished with mint.

COOK'S TIP
Most couscous is now the ready-cooked variety, which can be cooked as above, but some types need steaming first, so check the package instructions.

NUTRITION NOTES

Per portion:	
Energy	95Kcals/397kJ
Fat	0.53g
Saturated fat	0.07g
Cholesterol	0
Fiber	0.29g

CORN KERNEL PANCAKES

These crisp pancakes are delicious to serve as a snack lunch, or as a light supper with a crisp mixed salad.

INGREDIENTS

Serves 4, makes about 12
1 cup self-rising flour
1 egg white
⅔ cup skim milk
7oz can corn kernels, drained
oil, for brushing
salt and black pepper
tomato chutney, to serve

2 Season the batter well and add the remaining corn.

1 Place the flour, egg white, and skim milk in a food processor or blender with half the corn and process until smooth.

3 Heat a frying pan and brush with oil. Drop in tablespoons of batter and cook until set. Turn over the pancakes and cook the other side until golden. Serve hot with tomato chutney.

NUTRITION NOTES
Per portion:
Energy	162Kcals/680kJ
Fat	0.89g
Saturated fat	0.14g
Cholesterol	0.75mg
Fiber	1.49g

BAKED POLENTA WITH TOMATOES

INGREDIENTS

Serves 4
3⅔ cups broth
scant 1¼ cups polenta (coarse corn-meal)
4 tbsp chopped fresh sage
1 tsp olive oil
2 beefsteak tomatoes, sliced
1 tbsp grated Parmesan cheese
salt and black pepper

1 Bring the broth to a boil in a large saucepan, then gradually stir in the polenta.

2 Continue stirring the polenta over moderate heat for about 5 minutes, until the mixture begins to come away from the sides of the pan. Stir in the chopped sage and season well, then spoon the polenta into a lightly oiled, shallow 9x13 in pan and spread evenly. Leave to cool.

3 Preheat the oven to 400°F. Cut the cooled polenta into 24 squares using a sharp knife.

4 Arrange the polenta overlapping with tomato slices in a lightly oiled, shallow ovenproof dish. Sprinkle with Parmesan and bake for 20 minutes, or until golden brown. Serve hot.

NUTRITION NOTES
Per portion:
Energy	200Kcals/842kJ
Fat	3.8g
Saturated fat	0.77g
Cholesterol	1.88mg
Fiber	1.71g

LEMON AND HERB RISOTTO CAKE

This unusual rice dish can be served as a main course with salad, or as a satisfying side dish. It's also good served cold, and packs well for picnics.

INGREDIENTS

Serves 4

1 small leek, thinly sliced
2½ cups chicken broth
1 cup short-grain rice
finely grated rind of 1 lemon
2 tbsp chopped fresh chives
2 tbsp chopped fresh parsley
¾ cup shredded mozzarella cheese
salt and black pepper
parsley and lemon wedges, to garnish

1 Preheat the oven to 400°F. Lightly oil a deep-sided 8½ in round, loose-bottomed cake pan.

2 Cook the leek in a large pan with 3 tbsp broth, stirring over moderate heat, to soften. Add the rice and the remaining broth.

3 Bring to a boil. Cover the pan and simmer gently, stirring occasionally, for about 20 minutes, or until all the liquid is absorbed.

4 Stir in the lemon rind, herbs, cheese, and seasoning. Spoon into the cake pan, cover with foil and bake for 30–35 minutes or until lightly browned. Turn out and serve in slices, garnished with parsley and lemon wedges.

COOK'S TIP
The best type of rice to choose for this recipe is the Italian round grain Arborio rice, which should not be rinsed before use.

NUTRITION NOTES

Per portion:

Energy	280Kcals/1176kJ
Fat	6.19g
Saturated fat	2.54g
Cholesterol	12.19mg
Fiber	0.9g

RICE WITH SEEDS AND SPICES

A change from plain boiled rice, and a colorful accompaniment to serve with spicy curries or broiled meats. Basmati rice gives the best texture and flavor, but you can use ordinary long-grain rice instead, if you prefer.

INGREDIENTS

Serves 4

1 tsp sunflower oil
½ tsp ground turmeric
6 cardamom pods, lightly crushed
1 tsp coriander seeds, lightly crushed
1 garlic clove, crushed
1 cup basmati rice
1⅔ cups broth
½ cup plain yogurt
1 tbsp toasted sunflower seeds
1 tbsp toasted sesame seeds
salt and black pepper
cilantro leaves, to garnish

1 Heat the oil in a nonstick pan and sauté the spices and garlic for about 1 minute, stirring all the time.

2 Add the rice and broth, bring to a boil, then cover and simmer for 15 minutes, or until just tender.

3 Stir in the yogurt and the toasted sunflower and sesame seeds. Adjust the seasoning and serve hot, garnished with cilantro leaves.

NUTRITION NOTES

Per portion:

Energy	243Kcals/1022kJ
Fat	5.5g
Saturated fat	0.73g
Cholesterol	1.15mg
Fiber	0.57g

COOK'S TIP
Seeds are particularly rich in minerals, so they are a good addition to all kinds of dishes. Light roasting will improve their flavor.

VEGETABLES AND SALADS

We're very lucky to have a huge variety of fresh vegetables available all year round these days, so there is no excuse for not making maximum use of them in every meal, whether they form the basis of the main course, or are served as an accompaniment to meat or fish dishes. Get out of that dull daily rut of the same old familiar vegetables and try pepping them up with unusual flavors – Brussels sprouts will never be the same again when you've cooked them Chinese-style, and if you thought roast potatoes were banned, try Rosemary Roasties. Take a fresh look at salads, too, and discover that they needn't be soaked in heavy, oily dressings. Tangy plain low fat yogurt dressings or mustard and honey mixtures are light, flavorful and low in fat.

Vegetable Ribbons

This may just tempt a few fussy eaters to eat up their vegetables!

Ingredients

Serves 4

3 medium carrots
3 medium zucchini
½ cup chicken broth
2 tbsp chopped fresh parsley
salt and black pepper

1 Using a vegetable peeler or sharp knife, cut the carrots and zucchini into thin ribbons.

2 Bring the broth to a boil in a large saucepan and add the carrots. Return the broth to a boil, then add the zucchini. Boil rapidly for 2–3 minutes, or until the vegetable ribbons are just tender.

3 Stir in the parsley, season lightly, and serve hot.

Nutrition Notes

Per portion:

Energy	35Kcals/144kJ
Fat	0.53g
Saturated fat	0.09g
Cholesterol	0
Fiber	2.19g

Veggie Burgers

Ingredients

Serves 4

4oz cup mushrooms, finely chopped
1 small onion, chopped
1 small zucchini, chopped
1 carrot, chopped
1oz unsalted peanuts or cashews
2 cups fresh bread crumbs
2 tbsp chopped fresh parsley
1 tsp yeast extract
salt and black pepper
fine oatmeal or flour, for shaping

1 Cook the mushrooms in a nonstick pan without oil, stirring, for 8–10 minutes to remove all the moisture.

2 Process the onion, zucchini, carrot, and nuts in a food processor until beginning to bind together.

3 Stir in the mushrooms, bread-crumbs, parsley, yeast extract, and seasoning to taste. With the oatmeal or flour, shape into four burgers. Chill.

4 Cook the burgers in a nonstick frying pan with very little oil or under a hot broiler for 8–10 minutes, turning once, until the burgers are cooked and golden brown. Serve hot with a crisp salad.

Nutrition Notes

Per portion:

Energy	126Kcals/530kJ
Fat	3.8g
Saturated fat	0.73g
Cholesterol	0
Fiber	2.21g

CRACKED WHEAT AND FENNEL

This salad incorporates both sweet and savory flavors. It can be served as a side-dish or as an appetizer with warm pita bread.

INGREDIENTS

Serves 4

¾ cup cracked wheat
1 large fennel bulb, finely chopped
4oz green beans, chopped and blanched
1 small orange
1 garlic clove, crushed
2 tbsp sunflower oil
1 tbsp white wine vinegar
salt and black pepper
½ red or orange bell pepper, seeded and finely chopped, to garnish

NUTRITION NOTES	
Per portion:	
Energy	180Kcals/755kJ
Fat	6.32 g
Saturated fat	0.8g
Cholesterol	0
Fiber	2.31g

1 Place the wheat in a bowl and cover with boiling water. Leave for about 10–15 minutes. Drain well and squeeze out any excess water.

2 While still slightly warm, stir in the chopped fennel and green beans. Finely grate the orange rind into a bowl. Peel and segment the orange and stir into the salad.

3 Add the crushed garlic to the orange rind, then add the sunflower oil, white wine vinegar, and seasoning to taste, and mix thoroughly. Pour the dressing over the salad, mix well. Chill the salad for 1–2 hours.

4 Serve the salad sprinkled with the chopped red or orange bell pepper.

COOK'S TIP
When buying green beans, choose young, crisp ones.

SWEET POTATO AND CARROT SALAD

INGREDIENTS

Serves 4

1 sweet potato, peeled and
*   roughly diced*
2 carrots, cut into thick
*   diagonal slices*
3 tomatoes
8–10 iceberg lettuce leaves
¾ cup canned chick-peas, drained

For the dressing
1 tbsp clear honey
6 tbsp plain low fat yogurt
½ tsp salt
1 tsp coarsely ground black pepper

For the garnish
1 tbsp walnuts
1 tbsp golden raisins
1 small onion, cut into rings

NUTRITION NOTES

Per portion:

Energy	176Kcals/741kJ
Fat	4.85g
Saturated fat	0.58g
Cholesterol	0.85mg

1 Place the potatoes in a large saucepan and cover with water. Bring to a boil and cook until soft but not mushy, cover the pan and set aside. Boil the carrots for a few minutes making sure they remain crunchy. Add to the sweet potatoes.

3 Slice the tops off the tomatoes, then scoop out and discard the seeds. Roughly chop the flesh.

5 For the dressing, blend together all the ingredients and beat together with a fork.

2 Drain the water from the sweet potatoes and carrots, and place together in a bowl.

4 Line a glass bowl with the lettuce leaves. Mix together the sweet potatoes, carrots, chick-peas and tomatoes, and place in the bowl.

6 Spoon the dressing over the salad or serve it in a separate bowl. Garnish the salad with the walnuts, golden raisins and onion rings.

Masala Mashed Potatoes

These potatoes are very versatile and will perk up any meal.

Ingredients

Serves 4

3 potatoes
1 tbsp chopped fresh mint and
  cilantro, mixed
1 tsp mango powder
1 tsp salt
1 tsp crushed black peppercorns
1 red chili, chopped
1 green chili, chopped
4 tbsp low fat margarine

Nutrition Notes

Per portion:

Energy	94Kcals/394kJ
Fat	5.8g
Saturated fat	1.25g
Cholesterol	0.84mg

1 Place the potatoes in a large saucepan and cover with water. Bring to a boil and cook until soft enough to be mashed. Drain, then mash well.

2 Blend together the mint, cilantro, mango powder, salt, peppercorns, chilis and margarine in a small bowl.

3 Stir the mixture into the mashed potatoes and stir together thoroughly with a fork.

4 Serve warm as an accompaniment to meat or vegetarian dishes.

Cook's Tip
Mango powder is available in specialist Indian stores.

Spicy Cabbage

An excellent vegetable accompaniment, this dish can also be served as a warm side salad.

Ingredients

Serves 4

4 tbsp low fat margarine
½ tsp white cumin seeds
3–8 dried red chilies, to taste
1 small onion, sliced
2½ cups shredded cabbage
2 carrots, grated
½ tsp salt
2 tbsp lemon juice

Nutrition Notes

Per portion:

Energy	92Kcals/384kJ
Fat	6.06g
Saturated fat	1.28g
Cholesterol	0.84mg

1 Melt the low fat margarine in a saucepan and fry the white cumin seeds and dried red chilies for about 30 seconds.

2 Add the sliced onion and fry for about 2 minutes. Add the cabbage and carrots, and stir-fry for 5 minutes more or until the cabbage is soft.

3 Finally, stir in the salt and lemon juice, and serve either hot or warm.

RED CABBAGE IN PORT AND RED WINE

A sweet and sour, spicy red cabbage dish, with the added crunch of walnuts.

NUTRITION NOTES

Per portion:

Energy	336Kcals/1409kJ
Fat	15.41g
Saturated fat	1.58g
Cholesterol	0
Fiber	4.31g

INGREDIENTS

Serves 6

1 tbsp walnut oil
1 onion, sliced
2 whole star anise
1 tsp ground cinnamon
pinch of ground cloves
5 cups finely shredded red cabbage
2 tbsp dark brown sugar
3 tbsp red wine vinegar
1¼ cups red wine
⅔ cup port
2 pears, cut into ½in cubes
⅔ cup raisins
½ cup walnut halves
salt and black pepper

1 Heat the oil in a large flameproof casserole. Add the onion and cook gently for about 5 minutes until softened.

2 Add the star anise, cinnamon, cloves and cabbage, and cook for 3 minutes more.

3 Stir in the sugar, vinegar, red wine and port. Cover the pan and simmer gently for 10 minutes, stirring occasionally.

4 Stir in the cubed pears and raisins, and cook for 10 minutes more or until the cabbage is tender. Season to taste. Mix in the walnut halves and serve immediately.

COOK'S TIP
If you are unable to buy pre-packaged walnut halves, buy whole ones and shell them.

CRUSTY LEEK AND CARROT GRATIN

Tender leeks are mixed with a creamy caraway sauce and given a crunchy carrot topping.

INGREDIENTS

Serves 4–6
1½lb leeks, cut into 2in pieces
⅔ cup vegetable broth or water
3 tbsp dry white wine
1 tsp caraway seeds
pinch of salt
1 cup skim milk, or as required
2 tbsp sunflower margarine
¼ cup flour

For the topping
2 cups fresh whole-wheat breadcrumbs
2 cups grated carrot
2 tbsp chopped fresh parsley
¾ cup coarsely grated Jarlsberg cheese
2 tbsp sliced almonds

NUTRITION NOTES

Per portion:
Energy	314Kcals/1320kJ
Fat	15.42g
Saturated fat	6.75g
Cholesterol	30.75mg
Fiber	6.98g

2 With a slotted spoon, transfer the leeks to an ovenproof dish. Boil the remaining liquid to half the original volume, then make up to 1½ cups with skim milk.

3 Preheat the oven to 350°F. Melt the sunflower margarine in a flameproof casserole, stir in the flour and cook without allowing it to color for about 1–2 minutes. Gradually add the broth and milk, stirring well after each addition, until you have a smooth sauce.

4 Simmer the sauce for about 5–6 minutes, stirring constantly until thickened and smooth, then pour the sauce over the leeks in the dish.

5 For the topping, mix all the ingredients together in a bowl and sprinkle over the leeks. Bake for about 20–25 minutes until golden.

1 Place the leeks in a large saucepan and add the broth or water, wine, caraway seeds and salt. Bring to a simmer, cover and cook for about 5–7 minutes until the leeks are just tender.

SPICY BAKED POTATOES

INGREDIENTS

Serves 2–4

2 large baking potatoes
1 tsp sunflower oil
1 small onion, finely chopped
1in piece fresh ginger root, grated
1 tsp ground cumin
1 tsp ground coriander
½ tsp ground turmeric
garlic salt
plain yogurt and fresh cilantro sprigs,
    to serve

1 Preheat the oven to 375°F. Prick the potatoes with a fork. Bake for 40 minutes, or until soft.

2 Cut the potatoes in half and scoop out the flesh. Heat the oil in a non-stick pan and sauté the onion for a few minutes to soften. Stir in the ginger, cumin, coriander, and turmeric.

3 Stir over low heat for about 2 minutes, then add the potato flesh, and garlic salt, to taste.

4 Cook the potato mixture for 2 minutes more, stirring occasionally. Spoon the mixture back into the potato shells and top each with a spoonful of plain yogurt and a sprig or two of fresh cilantro. Serve hot.

NUTRITION NOTES

Per portion:

Energy	212Kcals/890kJ
Fat	2.54g
Saturated fat	0.31g
Cholesterol	0.4mg
Fiber	3.35g

TWO BEANS PROVENÇAL

INGREDIENTS

Serves 4

1 tsp olive oil
1 small onion, finely chopped
1 garlic clove, crushed
8oz haricot verts beans
8oz green beans
2 tomatoes, peeled and chopped
salt and black pepper

NUTRITION NOTES

Per portion:

Energy	68Kcals/286kJ
Fat	1.76g
Saturated fat	0.13g
Cholesterol	0
Fibre	5.39g

1 Heat the oil in a heavy-based, or nonstick, pan and sauté the chopped onion over medium heat until softened but not browned.

2 Add the garlic, both the beans, and the tomatoes, then season well and cover tightly.

3 Cook over fairly low heat, shaking the pan occasionally, for about 30 minutes, or until the beans are tender. Serve hot.

SPRING VEGETABLE STIR-FRY

A colorful, dazzling medley of fresh, delicious and sweet young vegetables.

NUTRITION NOTES	
Per portion:	
Energy	106Kcals/444kJ
Fat	4.38g
Saturated fat	0.63g
Cholesterol	0
Fiber	3.86g

INGREDIENTS

Serves 4

1 tbsp peanut oil
1 garlic clove, sliced
1in piece fresh ginger root, finely
   chopped
2 cups baby carrots
4oz patty-pan squash
1¼ cups baby corn
4oz green beans, topped
   and tailed
1¼ cups sugar-snap peas, topped
   and tailed
4oz young asparagus, cut into
   3in pieces
8 scallions, trimmed and cut into
   2in pieces
4oz cherry tomatoes

For the dressing

juice of 2 limes
1 tbsp clear honey
1 tbsp soy sauce
1 tsp sesame oil

1 Heat the peanut oil in a wok or large frying pan. Add the garlic and ginger and stir-fry for about 1 minute.

2 Add the carrots, patty-pan squash, baby corn and beans, and stir-fry for 3–4 minutes more.

3 Add the sugar-snap peas, asparagus, scallions and cherry tomatoes, and stir-fry for 1–2 minutes more.

4 For the dressing, mix all the ingredients together and add to the pan.

5 Stir well, then cover the pan. Cook for 2–3 minutes more until the vegetables are just tender but still crisp.

BEET AND CELERY ROOT GRATIN

INGREDIENTS

Serves 6

12oz raw beets
12oz celery root
4 thyme sprigs
6 juniper berries, crushed
½ cup fresh orange juice
½ cup vegetable broth
salt and black pepper

NUTRITION NOTES

Per portion:

Energy	37Kcals/157kJ
Fat	0.31g
Saturated fat	0
Cholesterol	0
Fiber	3.28g

1 Preheat the oven to 375°F. Peel and slice the beets very finely. Quarter and peel the celery root and slice very finely.

2 Fill a 10in diameter cast iron or ovenproof frying pan with layers of beet and celery root slices, sprinkling with the thyme, juniper and seasoning between each layer.

3 Mix the orange juice and broth together and pour over the gratin. Place over a medium heat and bring to a boil. Boil for about 2 minutes.

4 Cover with foil and place in the oven for about 15–20 minutes. Remove the foil and raise the oven temperature to 400°F. Cook for about 10 minutes more until tender. Serve garnished with a few extra crushed juniper berries and a sprig of thyme, if you like.

BOMBAY SPICED POTATOES

This Indian potato dish uses a wonderfully aromatic mixture of whole and ground spices. Look out for mustard and black onion seeds in specialist food stores.

INGREDIENTS

Serves 4

4 large potatoes, cut into chunks
4 tbsp sunflower oil
1 garlic clove, finely chopped
2 tsp brown mustard seeds
1 tsp black onion seeds (optional)
1 tsp turmeric
1 tsp ground cumin
1 tsp ground cilantro
1 tsp fennel seeds
good squeeze of lemon juice
salt and black pepper
chopped fresh cilantro and lemon
    wedges, to garnish

1 Bring a saucepan of salted water to a boil, add the potatoes and simmer for about 4 minutes, until just tender. Drain well.

2 Heat the oil in a large frying pan and add the garlic along with all the whole and ground spices. Fry gently for about 1–2 minutes, stirring until the mustard seeds start to pop.

3 Add the potatoes and stir-fry over a moderate heat for about 5 minutes, until heated through and well coated with the spicy oil.

4 Season well and sprinkle over the lemon juice. Garnish with chopped cilantro and lemon wedges. Serve as an accompaniment to curries or other strong-flavored dishes.

NUTRITION NOTES

Per portion:

Energy	373kcals/1149kJ
Fat	12.49g
Saturated fat	1.49g
Cholesterol	0
Fiber	2.65g

SPANISH CHILI POTATOES

INGREDIENTS

Serves 4

2¼lb new or salad potatoes
2 tbsp olive oil
1 onion, finely chopped
2 garlic cloves, crushed
1 tbsp tomato paste
7oz can chopped tomatoes
1 tbsp red wine vinegar
2–3 small dried red chilies, seeded and
    finely chopped, or 1–2 tsp hot chili
    powder
1 tsp paprika
salt and black pepper
flat leaf parsley sprig, to garnish

NUTRITION NOTES

Per portion:

Energy	301Kcals/1266kJ
Fat	12.02g
Saturated fat	1.6g
Cholesterol	0
Fiber	3.54g

1 Halve the potatoes if large, then place in a large saucepan and cover with water. Bring to a boil for about 10–12 minutes or until just tender. Drain well and leave to cool, then cut in half and reserve.

2 Heat the oil in a large pan and add the onions and garlic. Fry gently for about 5–6 minutes, until just softened. Stir in the next five ingredients, and simmer for about 5 minutes.

3 Add the potatoes and mix into the sauce mixture until well coated. Cover and simmer gently for about 8–10 minutes, or until the potatoes are tender. Season well and transfer to a warmed serving dish. Serve garnished with a sprig of flat leaf parsley.

BROCCOLI-CAULIFLOWER GRATIN

Broccoli and cauliflower make an attractive combination, and this dish is much lighter than the classic cheese sauce.

INGREDIENTS

Serves 4
1 small cauliflower (about 9oz)
1 small head broccoli (about 9oz)
½ cup plain low fat yogurt
1 cup shredded low fat Cheddar cheese
1 tsp whole-grain mustard
2 tbsp whole-wheat bread crumbs
salt and black pepper

1 Break the cauliflower and broccoli into florets and cook in lightly salted, boiling water for 8–10 minutes, until just tender. Drain well and transfer to a flameproof dish.

2 Mix together the yogurt, shredded cheese, and mustard, then season the mixture with pepper and spoon over the cauliflower and broccoli.

3 Sprinkle the bread crumbs over the top and place under a broiler until golden brown. Serve hot.

COOK'S TIP
When preparing the cauliflower and broccoli, discard the tougher part of the stalk, then break the florets into even-sized pieces, so they cook evenly.

NUTRITION NOTES

Per portion:

Energy	144Kcals/601kJ
Fat	6.5g
Saturated fat	3.25g
Cholesterol	16.5mg
Fiber	3.25g

WATERCRESS AND POTATO SALAD

New potatoes are equally good hot or cold, and this colorful, nutritious salad is an ideal way of making the most of them.

INGREDIENTS

Serves 4

1 lb small new potatoes, unpeeled
1 bunch watercress
1½ cups cherry tomatoes, halved
2 tbsp pumpkin seeds
3 tbsp low fat fromage frais
1 tbsp cider vinegar
1 tsp brown sugar
salt and paprika

1 Cook the potatoes in lightly salted, boiling water until just tender, then drain and leave to cool.

2 Toss together the potatoes, watercress, tomatoes, and pumpkin seeds.

3 Place the fromage frais, vinegar, sugar, salt, and paprika in a screwtop jar and shake well to mix. Pour over the salad just before serving.

NUTRITION NOTES

Per portion:

Energy	150Kcals/630kJ
Fat	4.15g
Saturated fat	0.81g
Cholesterol	0.11mg
Fiber	2.55g

COOK'S TIP
If you are packing this salad for a picnic, take the dressing in the jar and toss in just before serving.

TRICOLOR SALAD

A refreshing salad that goes well with broiled meats or fish. Alternatively, arrange it prettily on individual plates and serve as a summer starter.

INGREDIENTS

Serves 4
2 medium cooked beet, diced
2 Belgian endives, sliced
1 large orange
4 tbsp plain low fat yogurt
2 tsp whole-grain mustard
salt and black pepper

1 Mix together the diced, cooked beet and sliced Belgian endive in a large serving bowl.

2 Finely grate the rind from the orange. With a sharp knife, remove all the peel and white pith. Cut out the segments, catching the juice in a bowl. Add the segments to the salad.

3 Add the orange rind, yogurt, mustard, and seasonings to the orange juice, mix thoroughly, then spoon over the salad.

COOK'S TIP
Fresh baby spinach leaves or rocket could be used in place of the Belgian endive, if you prefer.

NUTRITION NOTES

Per portion:

Energy	41Kcals/172kJ
Fat	0.6g
Saturated fat	0.08g
Cholesterol	0.6mg
Fiber	1.42g

ROASTED BELL PEPPER SALAD

This colorful salad is very easy and can be made up to a day in advance, as the sharp-sweet dressing mingles with the mild pepper flavors.

INGREDIENTS

Serves 4
3 large red, green and yellow bell
* peppers, halved and seeded*
4oz feta cheese, diced or crumbled
1 tbsp sherry vinegar or red wine
* vinegar*
1 tbsp clear honey
salt and black pepper

1 Arrange the bell pepper halves in a single layer, skin side up, on a baking sheet. Place the bell peppers under a hot broiler until the skin is blackened and beginning to blister.

2 Lift the peppers into a plastic bag and close the end. Leave until cool, then peel off and discard the skin.

3 Arrange the bell peppers on a platter and scatter over the cheese. Mix together the vinegar, honey, and seasonings, then sprinkle over the salad. Chill until ready to serve.

NUTRITION NOTES

Per portion:

Energy	110Kcals/462kJ
Fat	6.15g
Saturated fat	3.65g
Cholesterol	20.13mg
Fiber	1.84g

MIDDLE-EASTERN VEGETABLE STEW

A spiced dish of mixed vegetables that can be served as a side dish or as a vegetarian main course. Children may prefer less chili.

INGREDIENTS

Serves 4–6
3 tbsp vegetable or chicken broth
1 green bell pepper, seeded and sliced
2 medium zucchini, sliced
2 medium carrots, sliced
2 celery sticks, sliced
2 medium potatoes, diced
14oz can chopped tomatoes
1 tsp chili powder
2 tbsp chopped fresh mint
1 tbsp ground cumin
14oz can chick peas, drained
salt and black pepper
mint sprigs, to garnish

1 Heat the vegetable or chicken broth in a large flameproof casserole until boiling, then add the sliced bell pepper, zucchini, carrot, and celery. Stir over high heat for 2–3 minutes, until the vegetables are just beginning to soften.

2 Add the potatoes, tomatoes, chili powder, mint, and cumin. Add the chick peas and bring to a boil.

3 Reduce the heat, cover the casserole, and simmer for 30 minutes, or until all the vegetables are tender. Season to taste with salt and pepper and serve hot, garnished with mint leaves.

COOK'S TIP
Chick peas are traditional in this type of Middle-Eastern dish, but if you prefer, red kidney beans or navy beans can be used instead.

NUTRITION NOTES

Per portion:
Energy	168Kcals/703kJ
Fat	3.16g
Saturated fat	0.12g
Cholesterol	0
Fiber	6.13g

SUMMER VEGETABLE BRAISE

Tender, young vegetables are ideal for quick cooking in a minimum of liquid. Use any mixture of the family's favorite vegetables, as long as they are of similar size.

INGREDIENTS

Serves 4
2½ cups baby carrots
2 cups sugar-snap peas or snow peas
1¼ cups baby corn
6 tbsp vegetable broth
2 tsp lime juice
salt and black pepper
chopped fresh parsley and snipped fresh
  chives, to garnish

1 Place the carrots, peas, and baby corn in a large heavy-based saucepan with the vegetable broth and lime juice. Bring to a boil.

2 Cover the pan and reduce the heat, then simmer for 6–8 minutes, shaking the pan occasionally, until the vegetables are just tender.

3 Season the vegetables to taste with salt and pepper, then stir in the chopped fresh parsley and snipped chives. Cook the vegetables for a few seconds more, stirring them once or twice until the herbs are well mixed, then serve at once, with broiled lamb chops or roast chicken.

COOK'S TIP
You can make this dish in the winter too, but cut larger, tougher vegetables into chunks and cook for slightly longer.

NUTRITION NOTES

Per portion:

Energy	36Kcals/152kJ
Fat	0.45g
Saturated fat	0
Cholesterol	0
Fiber	2.35g

ROSEMARY ROASTIES

These unusual roast potatoes use far less fat than traditional roast potatoes, and because they still have their skins they not only absorb less oil but have more flavor too.

— INGREDIENTS —

Serves 4
2 lb small red potatoes
2 tsp walnut or sunflower oil
2 tbsp fresh rosemary leaves
salt and paprika

1 Preheat the oven to 475°F. Leave the potatoes whole with the peel on, or if large, cut in half. Place the potatoes in a large pan of cold water and bring to a boil. Drain well.

2 Drizzle the walnut or sunflower oil over the potatoes and shake the pan to coat them evenly.

3 Tip the potatoes into a shallow roasting pan. Sprinkle with rosemary, salt, and paprika. Roast for 30 minutes or until crisp. Serve hot.

— NUTRITION NOTES —

Per portion:
Energy	205Kcals/865kJ
Fat	2.22g
Saturated fat	0.19g
Cholesterol	0
Fiber	3.25g

BAKED ZUCCHINI IN TOMATO SAUCE

— INGREDIENTS —

Serves 4
1 tsp olive oil
3 large zucchini, thinly sliced
½ small red onion, finely chopped
1¼ cups tomato sauce
2 tbsp chopped fresh thyme
garlic salt and black pepper
fresh thyme sprigs, to garnish

1 Preheat the oven to 375°F. Brush an ovenproof dish with olive oil. Arrange half the zucchini and onion in the dish.

2 Spoon half the tomato sauce over the vegetables and sprinkle with some of the fresh thyme, then season to taste with garlic salt and pepper.

3 Arrange the remaining zucchini and onion in the dish on top of the sauce, then season to taste with more garlic salt and pepper. Spoon over the remaining sauce and spread evenly.

4 Cover the dish with foil, then bake for 40–45 minutes, or until the zucchini is tender. Garnish with sprigs of thyme and serve hot.

— NUTRITION NOTES —

Per portion:
Energy	49Kcals/205kJ
Fat	1.43g
Saturated fat	0.22g
Cholesterol	0
Fiber	1.73g

CHINESE SPROUTS

If you are bored with plain boiled Brussels sprouts, try pepping them up with this unusual stir-fried method, which uses the minimum of oil.

INGREDIENTS

Serves 4
1 lb Brussels sprouts, shredded
1 tsp sesame or sunflower oil
2 scallions, sliced
½ tsp Chinese five-spice powder
1 tbsp light soy sauce

1 Trim the Brussels sprouts, then shred them finely using a large sharp knife or shred in a food processor.

2 Heat the oil and add the sprouts and onions, then stir-fry for about 2 minutes, without browning.

3 Stir in the five-spice powder and soy sauce, then cook, stirring, for 2–3 minutes more, until just tender.

4 Serve hot, with broiled meats or fish, or Chinese dishes.

COOK'S TIP
Brussels sprouts are rich in Vitamin C, and this is a good way to cook them to preserve the vitamins. Larger sprouts cook particularly well by this method, and cabbage can also be cooked this way.

NUTRITION NOTES

Per portion:

Energy	58Kcals/243kJ
Fat	2.38g
Saturated fat	0.26g
Cholesterol	0
Fiber	4.67g

LEMONY VEGETABLE PARCELS

INGREDIENTS

Serves 4

2 medium carrots
1 small rutabaga
1 large parsnip
1 leek, sliced
finely grated rind of ½ lemon
1 tbsp lemon juice
1 tbsp whole-grain mustard
1 tsp walnut or sunflower oil
salt and black pepper

1 Preheat the oven to 375°F. Peel the root vegetables and cut into ½ in cubes. Place in a large bowl, then add the sliced leek.

2 Stir the lemon rind and juice and the mustard into the vegetables and mix well, then season to taste.

3 Cut four 12 in squares of nonstick baking paper and brush them lightly with the oil.

4 Divide the vegetables among them. Roll up the paper from one side, then twist the ends firmly to seal.

5 Place the parcels on a baking sheet and bake for 50–55 minutes, or until the vegetables are just tender. Serve hot, with roast or broiled meats.

NUTRITION NOTES

Per portion	
Energy	78Kcals/326kJ
Fat	2.06g
Saturated fat	0.08g
Cholesterol	0
Fiber	5.15g

New Potato Parcels

These delicious potatoes may be cooked in individual portions.

INGREDIENTS

Serves 4

16–20 very small potatoes in their skins
3 tbsp olive oil
1–2 sprigs each of thyme, tarragon
    and oregano, or 1 tbsp mixed
    dried herbs
salt and black pepper

NUTRITION NOTES

Per portion:

Energy	206Kcals/866kJ
Fat	11.49g
Saturated fat	1.54g
Cholesterol	0
Fiber	1.5g

1 Preheat the oven to 400°F. Lightly grease one large sheet or four small sheets of foil.

2 Put the potatoes in a large bowl and add in the rest of the ingredients and seasoning. Mix well so the potatoes are thoroughly coated.

3 Put the potatoes on the foil and seal up the parcel(s). Place on a cookie sheet and bake for about 40–50 minutes. The potatoes will stay warm for quite some time if left wrapped up.

COOK'S TIP
This dish can also be cooked on a barbecue, if you like.

Stir-fried Florets with Hazelnuts

INGREDIENTS

Serves 4

1½ cups cauliflower florets
1½ cups broccoli florets
1 tbsp sunflower oil
¼ cup hazelnuts, finely chopped
¼ red chili, finely chopped, or 1 tsp
    chili powder (optional)
4 tbsp very low fat sour cream or
    ricotta cheese
salt and black pepper
a little paprika, to garnish

NUTRITION NOTES

Per portion:

Energy	146Kcals/614kJ
Fat	11.53g
Saturated fat	0.94g
Cholesterol	0.15mg
Fiber	2.84g

1 Make sure the cauliflower and broccoli florets are all of an even size. Heat the oil in a saucepan or wok and toss the florets over a high heat for 1 minute.

2 Reduce the heat and continue stir-frying for 5 minutes more, then add the hazelnuts, chili, if using, and seasoning to taste.

3 Fry the cauliflower and broccoli florets until crisp and nearly tender, then stir in the sour cream or ricotta cheese and just heat through. Serve at once, sprinkled with the paprika.

COOK'S TIP
The crisper these florets are, the better, so cook them just long enough to make them piping hot, and give them time to absorb all the flavors.

HOT DESSERTS

Dessert lovers will be glad to learn that desserts need not be taboo for low fat diets. There are lots of ways to cook quite substantial desserts without the need for rich, high-fat mixtures. Classic crisps can be made a little less sinful and far more exciting by adding less fat and more crunch in the form of oatmeal or nuts. Skim or semi-skim milk, with a little whisked egg white, will lighten a milk pudding, and egg whites can be used in place of whole eggs for pancakes or cakes. For a change, try an unusual couscous or bread crumb mixture instead of a heavy sponge pudding. Even a delicious, sticky Gingerbread Upside Down Cake can be made with just a little oil and the minimum of eggs, with no loss of appeal.

FLOATING ISLANDS IN HOT PLUM SAUCE

An unusual pudding that is simpler to make than it looks. The plum sauce can be made in advance, and reheated just before you cook the meringues.

INGREDIENTS

Serves 4
1lb red plums
1¼ cups apple juice
2 egg whites
2 tbsp apple juice concentrate
freshly grated nutmeg, to sprinkle

NUTRITION NOTES

Per portion:	
Energy	90Kcals/380kJ
Fat	0.3g
Saturated fat	0
Cholesterol	0
Fiber	1.69g

2 Bring to a boil, then cover and simmer gently until the plums have become tender.

3 Meanwhile, place the egg whites in a clean, dry bowl and whisk them until they hold soft peaks.

1 Halve the plums and remove the pits. Place them in a wide saucepan, with the apple juice.

4 Gradually whisk in the apple juice concentrate, whisking until the meringue holds fairly firm peaks.

5 Using a tablespoon, scoop the meringue mixture into the gently simmering plum sauce. You may need to cook the "islands" in two batches.

6 Cover and simmer gently for about 2–3 minutes, until the meringues are set. Serve immediately, sprinkled with a little freshly grated nutmeg.

> **COOK'S TIP**
> A bottle of apple juice concentrate is a useful storecupboard sweetener, but if you don't have any, use a little clear honey instead.

CHUNKY APPLE BAKE

This filling, economical family dessert is a good way to use up slightly stale bread – any type of bread will do, but whole-wheat is richest in fiber.

INGREDIENTS

Serves 4
1lb cooking apples
3oz whole-wheat bread, without crusts
½ cup cottage cheese
3 tbsp light brown sugar
⅞ cup skim milk
1 tsp raw sugar

NUTRITION NOTES

Per portion:
Energy	163Kcals/687kJ
Fat	1.75g
Saturated fat	0.84g
Cholesterol	4.74mg

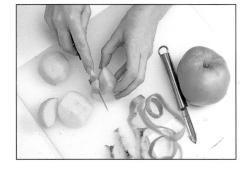

1 Preheat the oven to 425°F. Peel the apples, cut them in quarters and remove the cores.

2 Roughly chop the apples into even-size pieces, about ½in across.

3 Cut the bread into ½in dice with a sharp knife.

4 Toss together the apples, bread, cottage cheese and light brown sugar.

5 Stir in the milk and then tip the mixture into a wide ovenproof dish. Sprinkle with the raw sugar.

6 Bake for about 30–35 minutes, or until golden brown and bubbling. Serve while still hot.

> **COOK'S TIP**
> You may need to adjust the amount of milk used; the staler the bread, the more milk it will absorb.

SNOW-CAPPED APPLES

INGREDIENTS

Serves 4

4 tart baking apples
6 tbsp orange marmalade or jam
2 egg whites
4 tbsp sugar

1 Preheat the oven to 350°F. Core the apples and score through the skins around the middle with a sharp knife.

2 Place in a wide ovenproof dish and spoon 1 tbsp marmalade into the center of each. Cover and bake for 35–40 minutes, or until tender.

3 Whisk the egg whites in a large bowl until stiff enough to hold soft peaks. Whisk in the sugar, then fold in the remaining marmalade.

4 Spoon the meringue over the apples, then return to the oven for 10–15 minutes, or until golden. Serve hot.

NUTRITION NOTES

Per portion:

Energy	165Kcals/394kJ
Fat	0.16g
Saturated fat	0
Cholesterol	0
Fiber	1.9g

STRAWBERRY AND APPLE TART

INGREDIENTS

Serves 4–6

1¼ cups self-rising flour
⅔ cup oatmeal
4 tbsp sunflower margarine
2 tart baking apples, about 1 lb total
  weight
2 cups strawberries, halved
4 tbsp sugar
1 tbsp cornstarch

1 Preheat the oven to 400°F. Mix together the flour and oatmeal in a large bowl and rub in the margarine evenly. Stir in just enough cold water to bind the mixture to a firm dough. Knead lightly until smooth.

2 Roll out the pastry and line a 9in loose-based tart pan. Trim the edges, prick the base, and line with baking paper and baking beans. Roll out the pastry trimmings and stamp out heart shapes using a cutter.

3 Bake the pastry shell for 10 minutes, remove paper and beans, and bake for 10–15 minutes or until golden brown. Bake the hearts until golden.

4 Peel, core, and slice the apples. Place in a pan with the strawberries, sugar, and cornstarch. Cover and cook gently, stirring, until the fruit is just tender. Spoon into the pastry shell and decorate with pastry hearts.

NUTRITION NOTES

Per portion:

Energy	382Kcals/1602kJ
Fat	11.93g
Saturated fat	2.18g
Cholesterol	0.88mg
Fiber	4.37g

GOLDEN GINGER COMPOTE

Warm, spicy and full of sun-ripened ingredients – this is the perfect winter dessert.

NUTRITION NOTES	
Per portion:	
Energy	196Kcals/825kJ
Fat	2.84g
Saturated fat	0.41g
Cholesterol	0
Fiber	6.82g

INGREDIENTS

Serves 4

2 cups kumquats
1¼ cups dried apricots
2 tbsp golden raisins
1⅔ cups water
1 orange
1in piece fresh ginger root
4 cardamom pods
4 cloves
2 tbsp clear honey
1 tbsp sliced almonds, toasted

1 Wash the kumquats and, if they are large, cut them in half. Place them in a saucepan with the apricots, golden raisins and water. Bring to a boil.

2 Pare the rind thinly from the orange, peel and grate the ginger, crush the cardamom pods and add to the pan, with the cloves.

3 Reduce the heat, cover the pan and simmer gently for about 30 minutes, or until the fruit is tender.

4 Squeeze the juice from the orange and add to the pan with honey to sweeten to taste, sprinkle with sliced almonds, and serve warm.

COOK'S TIP
Use ready-to-eat dried apricots, but reduce the liquid to 1¼ cups, and add 5 minutes before the end.

NECTARINES WITH SPICED RICOTTA

This easy dessert is good at any time of year – use canned peach halves if fresh nectarines or peaches are out of season.

INGREDIENTS

Serves 4
4 ripe nectarines or peaches
1 tbsp light brown sugar
½ cup ricotta cheese
½ tsp ground star anise, to decorate

NUTRITION NOTES

Per portion:

Energy	92Kcals/388kJ
Fat	3.27g
Saturated fat	0
Cholesterol	14.38mg
Fiber	1.65g

1 Cut the nectarines, or peaches if using, in half and remove the pits. Do this carefully with a sharp knife and a steady hand.

2 Arrange the nectarines or peaches, cut-side upwards, in a wide flameproof dish or on a baking sheet.

3 Place the ricotta cheese into a small mixing bowl. Stir the light brown sugar into the ricotta cheese. Using a teaspoon, spoon equal amounts of the mixture into the hollow of each nectarine or peach half.

4 Sprinkle with the star anise. Cook under a moderately hot broiler for 6–8 minutes, or until the nectarines or peaches are hot. Serve warm.

COOK'S TIP
Star anise has a warm, rich flavor – if you can't get it, use ground cloves or ground allspice as an alternative.

SPICED RED FRUIT COMPOTE

Serves 4

4 ripe red plums, halved
2 cups strawberries, halved
1¾ cups raspberries
2 tbsp brown sugar
2 tbsp cold water
1 cinnamon stick
3 pieces star anise
6 cloves

── **NUTRITION NOTES** ──

Per portion:	
Energy	90Kcals/375kJ
Fat	0.32g
Saturated fat	0
Cholesterol	0
Fiber	3.38g

1 Place the plums, strawberries, and raspberies in a heavy-based pan with the sugar and water.

2 Add the cinnamon stick, star anise, and cloves to the pan and heat gently, without boiling, until the sugar dissolves and the fruit juices run.

3 Cover the pan and leave the fruit to infuse over very low heat for about 5 minutes. Remove the spices from the compote before serving warm, with plain yogurt or fromage frais.

RHUBARB SPIRAL COBBLER

Serves 4

1½ lb rhubarb, sliced
4 tbsp granulated sugar
3 tbsp orange juice
1⅓ cups self-rising flour
2 tbsp superfine sugar
about 1 cup plain yogurt
grated rind of 1 medium orange
2 tbsp raw sugar
1 tsp ground ginger

1 Preheat the oven to 400°F. Cook the rhubarb, sugar, and orange juice in a covered pan until tender. Tip into an ovenproof dish.

2 To make the topping, mix the flour, superfine sugar, and enough yogurt to bind to a soft dough.

3 Roll out on a floured surface to a 10in square. Mix the orange rind, raw sugar, and ginger, then sprinkle this over the dough.

4 Roll up quite tightly, then cut into about 10 slices using a sharp knife. Arrange the slices over the rhubarb.

5 Bake in the oven for 15–20 minutes, or until the spirals are puffed and golden brown. Serve warm, with ordinary or frozen yogurt.

── **NUTRITION NOTES** ──

Per portion:	
Energy	320Kcals/1343kJ
Fat	1.2g
Saturated fat	0.34g
Cholesterol	2mg
Fiber	3.92g

Coconut and Lemon Dumplings

INGREDIENTS

Serves 4

For the dumplings
⅓ cup cottage cheese
1 egg white
2 tbsp low fat margarine
1 tbsp light brown sugar
2 tbsp self-raising whole-wheat flour
finely grated rind of ½ lemon
2 tbsp shredded coconut, toasted, plus
  extra, to decorate

For the sauce
8oz can apricot halves in natural juice
1 tbsp lemon juice

NUTRITION NOTES

Per portion:
Energy	162Kcals/681kJ
Fat	9.5g
Saturated fat	5.47g
Cholesterol	33.69mg
Fiber	2.21g

1 Half-fill a steamer with boiling water and put it on to boil, or place a heatproof dish over a saucepan of boiling water.

2 Beat together the cottage cheese, egg white and margarine.

3 Stir in the sugar, flour, lemon rind and coconut, mixing evenly to form a fairly firm dough.

4 Place eight to twelve spoonfuls of the mixture in the steamer or on the dish, leaving space between them.

5 Cover the steamer or pan tightly with a lid or a plate and steam for about 10 minutes, until the dumplings have risen and are firm to the touch.

6 Meanwhile make the sauce: put the apricots in a food processor or blender, and process until smooth. Stir in the lemon juice. Pour into a small pan and heat until boiling, then serve with the dumplings. Sprinkle with extra coconut to decorate.

BAKED APPLES IN HONEY AND LEMON

A classic mix of flavors in a healthy, traditional family dessert. Serve warm, with skim milk custard.

INGREDIENTS

Serves 4
4 cooking apples
1 tbsp clear honey
grated rind and juice of 1 lemon
2 tbsp low fat margarine

NUTRITION NOTES

Per portion:
Energy	71Kcals/299kJ
Fat	1.69g
Saturated fat	0.37g
Cholesterol	0.23mg
Fiber	1.93g

COOK'S TIP
Apples are divided into dessert (or eating) and cooking apples. While cooking apples can only be used for culinary purposes because they have a sour taste, some dessert apples, especially if firm, can be used in cooking. Look for smooth skinned apples and avoid any with brown bruises.

2 With a cannelle or sharp knife, cut lines through the apple skin at intervals and place in an ovenproof dish.

4 Spoon the mixture into the apples and cover the dish with foil or a lid. Bake for about 40–45 minutes, or until the apples are tender. Serve with custard made from skim milk.

1 Preheat the oven to 350°F. Remove the cores from the apples, leaving them whole.

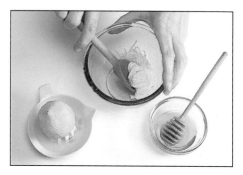

3 Mix together the honey, lemon rind and juice, and low fat margarine.

COOK'S TIP
This recipe can also be cooked in the microwave to save time. Place the apples in a microwave-safe dish and cover them with a lid or pierced plastic wrap. Microwave on FULL POWER (100%) for about 9–10 minutes.

CRISPY PEACH BAKE

A golden, crisp-crusted, family dessert that's made in minutes, from storecupboard ingredients.

INGREDIENTS

Serves 4

14½oz can peach slices in juice
2 tbsp golden raisins
1 cinnamon stick
strip of fresh orange rind
2 tbsp low fat margarine
1½ cups cornflakes
1 tbsp sesame seeds

COOK'S TIP
If you don't have a cinnamon stick, sprinkle in about ½ tsp ground cinnamon instead.

1 Drain the peaches, reserving the juice, and arrange the peach slices in a shallow ovenproof dish.

2 Preheat the oven to 400°F. Place the peach juice, golden raisins, cinnamon stick and orange rind in a saucepan and bring to a boil. Simmer, uncovered, for about 3–4 minutes, to reduce the liquid by about half. Remove the cinnamon stick and orange rind, and spoon the syrup and golden raisins over the peaches.

3 Melt the margarine in a small pan and stir in the cornflakes and sesame seeds.

4 Spread the cornflake mixture over the fruit. Bake for about 15–20 minutes, or until the topping is crisp and golden. Serve hot.

BAKED BLACKBERRY CHEESECAKE

This light cheesecake is best made with wild blackberries, but cultivated ones will do. You can also substitute them for other soft fruit such as raspberries or loganberries.

── INGREDIENTS ──

Serves 5
¾ *cup cottage cheese*
⅔ *cup plain low fat yogurt*
1 tbsp whole-wheat flour
2 tbsp golden caster sugar
1 egg
1 egg white
finely grated rind and juice of ½ lemon
2 cups blackberries

── NUTRITION NOTES ──

Per portion:	
Energy	94Kcals/394kJ
Fat	1.67g
Saturated fat	1.03g
Cholesterol	5.75mg
Fiber	1.71g

1 Preheat the oven to 350°F. Lightly grease and line the base of a 7in cake pan.

2 Whizz the cottage cheese in a food processor or blender until smooth, or rub it through a strainer.

3 Add the yogurt, flour, sugar, egg and egg white, and mix. Add the lemon rind and juice, and blackberries, reserving a few for decoration.

4 Tip the mixture into the prepared pan and bake it for about 30–35 minutes, or until just set. Turn off the oven and leave for 30 minutes.

5 Run a knife around the edge of the cheesecake, and then turn it out.

6 Remove the lining paper and place the cheesecake on a warm serving plate. Decorate with the reserved blackberries and serve it warm.

COOK'S TIP
If you prefer to use canned blackberries, choose those preserved in natural juice and drain the fruit well before adding it to the cheesecake mixture. The juice may be served with the cheesecake, but this will increase the total calories.

HOT PLUM BATTER

Other fruits can be used in place of plums, depending on the season. Canned black cherries are also a convenient pantry substitute.

INGREDIENTS

Serves 4
1 lb ripe red plums, quartered and pitted
⅞ cup skim milk
4 tbsp skim milk powder
1 tbsp brown sugar
1 tsp vanilla extract
3oz self-rising flour
2 egg whites
confectioners' sugar, to sprinkle

1 Preheat the oven to 425°F. Lightly oil a wide, shallow ovenproof dish and add the plums.

2 Pour the milk, milk powder, sugar, vanilla, flour, and egg whites into a food processor. Process until smooth.

3 Pour the batter over the plums. Bake for 25–30 minutes, or until puffed and golden. Sprinkle with confectioners' sugar and serve hot.

NUTRITION NOTES

Per portion:

Energy	195Kcals/816kJ
Fat	0.48g
Saturated fat	0.12g
Cholesterol	2.8mg
Fiber	2.27g

GLAZED APRICOT PUDDING

British-style puddings are usually very high in saturated fat, but this one uses the minimum of oil and no eggs.

INGREDIENTS

Serves 4
2 tsp golden syrup
14oz can apricot halves in fruit juice
1¼ cup self-rising flour
1½ cups fresh bread crumbs
⅔ cup brown sugar
1 tsp ground cinnamon
2 tbsp sunflower oil
¼ cup skim milk

1 Preheat the oven to 350°F. Lightly oil a cup pudding bowl. Spoon in the syrup.

2 Drain the apricots and reserve the juice. Arrange about 8 halves in the basin. Purée the rest of the apricots with the juice and set aside.

3 Mix the flour, bread crumbs, sugar, and cinnamon, then beat in the oil and milk. Spoon into the bowl and bake for 50–55 minutes, or until firm and golden. Turn out and serve with the puréed fruit as a sauce.

NUTRITION NOTES

Per portion:

Energy	364Kcals/1530kJ
Fat	6.47g
Saturated fat	0.89g
Cholesterol	0.88mg
Fiber	2.37g

Cherry Crêpes

Serves 4
½ cup flour
⅓ cup whole-wheat flour
pinch of salt
1 egg white
⅔ cup skim milk
⅔ cup water
1 tbsp sunflower oil, for frying
low fat ricotta cheese, to serve

For the filling
15oz can black cherries in juice
1½ tsp arrowroot

— Nutrition Notes —

Per portion:
Energy	173Kcals/725kJ
Fat	3.33g
Saturated fat	0.44g
Cholesterol	0.75mg
Fiber	2.36g

1 Sift the flours and salt into a bowl, adding any bran left in the sifter to the bowl at the end.

2 Make a well in the center of the flour and add the egg white. Gradually beat in the milk and water, whisking hard until all the liquid is incorporated and the batter is smooth and bubbly.

3 Heat a nonstick frying pan with a small amount of oil until the pan is very hot. Pour in just enough batter to cover the base of the pan, swirling the pan to cover the base evenly.

4 Cook until the crêpe is set and golden, and then turn to cook the other side. Remove to a sheet of paper towel and then cook the remaining batter, to make about eight pancakes.

5 For the filling, drain the cherries, reserving the juice. Blend about 2 tbsp of the juice from the can of cherries with the arrowroot in a saucepan. Stir in the rest of the juice. Heat gently, stirring, until boiling. Stir over a moderate heat for about 2 minutes, until thickened and clear.

6 Add the cherries to the sauce and stir until thoroughly heated. Spoon the cherries into the crêpes and fold them into quarters.

Cook's Tip
If fresh cherries are in season, cook them gently in enough apple juice just to cover them, and then thicken the juice with arrowroot as in Step 5. The basic crêpes will freeze very successfully between layers of paper towel or waxed paper.

SOUFFLÉED RICE PUDDING

Serves 4

¼ cup short grain rice
3 tbsp clear honey
3⅔ cups skim milk
1 vanilla bean or ½ tsp
  vanilla extract
2 egg whites
1 tsp freshly grated nutmeg

NUTRITION NOTES

Per portion:
Energy	163Kcals/683kJ
Fat	0.62g
Saturated fat	0.16g
Cholesterol	3.75mg
Fiber	0.08g

1 Place the rice, honey and milk in a heavy or nonstick saucepan, and bring the milk to a boil. Add the vanilla bean, if using it.

2 Reduce the heat and put the lid on the pan. Leave to simmer gently for about 1–1¼ hours, stirring occasionally to prevent sticking, until most of the liquid has been absorbed.

3 Remove the vanilla bean from the rice, or if using vanilla extract, add this to the rice mixture now. Preheat the oven to 425°F.

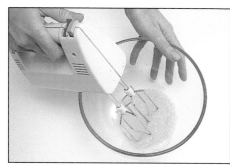

4 Place the egg whites in a clean, dry bowl and whisk them until they hold soft peaks.

5 Using either a large metal spoon or a plastic spatula, carefully fold the egg whites evenly into the rice and milk mixture and tip into a 4 cup ovenproof dish.

6 Sprinkle with grated nutmeg and bake for about 15–20 minutes, until the pudding is well risen and golden brown. Serve hot.

COOK'S TIP
Be very careful when simmering skim milk. With so little fat, it tends to boil over very easily. Use semi-skim if you wish.

CRUNCHY GOOSEBERRY CRISP

Gooseberries are perfect for traditional family desserts like this one. When they are out of season, other fruits such as apple, plums, or rhubarb could be used instead.

INGREDIENTS

Serves 4
5 cups gooseberries
4 tbsp granulated sugar
1 cup oatmeal
¾ cup whole-wheat flour
4 tbsp sunflower oil
4 tbsp raw sugar
2 tbsp chopped walnuts
plain yogurt, to serve

1 Preheat the oven to 400°F. Place the gooseberries in a pan with the granulated sugar. Cover and cook over low heat for 10 minutes, until the gooseberries are just tender. Tip into an ovenproof dish.

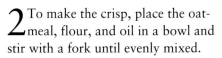

2 To make the crisp, place the oatmeal, flour, and oil in a bowl and stir with a fork until evenly mixed.

3 Stir in the raw sugar and walnuts, then spread evenly over the gooseberries. Bake for 25–30 minutes, or until golden and bubbling. Serve hot with yogurt.

COOK'S TIP
The best cooking gooseberries are the early small, firm green ones.

NUTRITION NOTES

Per portion:
Energy	422Kcals/1770kJ
Fat	18.5g
Saturated fat	2.32g
Cholesterol	0
Fiber	5.12g

GINGERBREAD UPSIDE-DOWN CAKE

The perfect warmer-upper on a
cold winter's day. This one is
quite quick to make and looks
very impressive.

INGREDIENTS

Serves 4 – 6
sunflower oil, for brushing
1 tbsp brown sugar
4 medium peaches, halved and pitted,
  or canned peach halves
8 walnut halves

For the base
½ cup whole-wheat flour
½ tsp baking soda
1½ tsp ground ginger
1 tsp ground cinnamon
½ cup brown sugar
1 egg
½ cup skim milk
¼ cup sunflower oil

1 Preheat the oven to 350°F. For the
topping, brush the base and sides
of a 9in round spring form cake pan
with oil. Sprinkle the sugar over the
base.

2 Arrange the peaches cut-side down in
the pan with a walnut half in each.

3 For the base, sift together the flour,
baking soda, ginger, and cinnamon,
then stir in the sugar. Beat together the
egg, milk and oil, then mix into the dry
ingredients until smooth.

4 Pour the mixture evenly over the
peaches and bake for 35–40
minutes, until firm to the touch. Turn
out onto a serving plate. Serve hot with
yogurt or low fat ice cream.

NUTRITION NOTES

Per portion:	
Energy	432Kcals/1812kJ
Fat	16.54g
Saturated fat	2.27g
Cholesterol	48.72mg
Fiber	4.79g

Plum Fila Pockets

Ingredients

Serves 4

½ cup low fat cream cheese
1 tbsp brown sugar
½ tsp ground cloves
8 large, firm plums, halved and pitted
8 sheets fila pastry
sunflower oil, for brushing
confectioners' sugar, to sprinkle

1 Preheat the oven to 425°F. Mix together the low fat cream cheese, sugar, and cloves.

2 Sandwich the plum halves back together in pairs with a spoonful of the cheese mixture.

3 Spread out the pastry and cut into 16 pieces, about 9in square. Brush one lightly with oil and place a second at a diagonal on top. Repeat with the remaining squares.

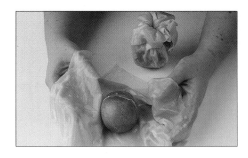

4 Place a plum on each pastry square, and pinch corners together. Place on baking sheet. Bake for 15–18 minutes, until golden, then dust with sugar.

Nutrition Notes

Per portion:

Energy	188Kcals/790kJ
Fat	1.87g
Saturated fat	0.27g
Cholesterol	0.29mg
Fiber	2.55g

Apple-Couscous Pudding

This unusual mixture makes a delicious family dessert with a rich fruity flavor, but virtually no fat.

Ingredients

Serves 4

2½ cups apple juice
⅔ cup couscous
¼ cup raisins
½ tsp mixed spice
1 large tart baking apple, peeled, cored, and sliced
2 tbsp raw sugar
plain low fat yogurt, to serve

1 Preheat the oven to 400°F. Place the apple juice, couscous, raisins, and spice in a pan and bring to a boil, stirring. Cover and simmer for 10–12 minutes, until all the liquid is absorbed.

2 Spoon half the couscous mixture into a 5 cup ovenproof dish and top with half the apple slices. Top with remaining couscous.

3 Arrange the remaining apple slices overlapping over the top and sprinkle with raw sugar. Bake for 25–30 minutes, or until golden brown. Serve hot, with yogurt.

Nutrition Notes

Per portion:

Energy	194Kcals/815kJ
Fat	0.58g
Saturated fat	0.09g
Cholesterol	0
Fiber	0.75g

FRUITY BREAD PUDDING

A delicious family favorite from grandmother's day, with a lighter, healthier touch.

INGREDIENTS

Serves 4

⅔ cup mixed dried fruit
⅔ cup apple juice
1¼ cups stale whole-wheat or white bread, diced
1 tsp cinnamon
1 large banana, sliced
⅔ cup skim milk
1 tbsp raw sugar
plain low fat yogurt, to serve

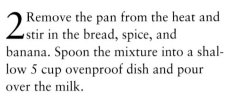

1 Preheat the oven to 400°F. Place the dried fruit in a small pan with the apple juice and bring to a boil.

2 Remove the pan from the heat and stir in the bread, spice, and banana. Spoon the mixture into a shallow 5 cup ovenproof dish and pour over the milk.

3 Sprinkle with raw sugar and bake for 25–30 minutes, until firm and golden brown. Serve hot or cold with plain yogurt.

COOK'S TIP
Different types of bread will absorb varying amounts of liquid, so you may need to adjust the amount of milk to allow for this.

NUTRITION NOTES

Per portion:

Energy	190Kcals/800kJ
Fat	0.89g
Saturated fat	0.21g
Cholesterol	0.75mg
Fiber	1.8g

SOUFFLÉED ORANGE SEMOLINA

Semolina has a reputation as a rather dull, sloppy pudding, but cooked like this you would hardly recognize it.

INGREDIENTS

Serves 4
¼ cup semolina flour
2½ cups low fat milk
2 tbsp brown sugar
1 large orange
1 egg white

1 Preheat the oven to 400°F. Place the semolina in a nonstick pan with the milk and sugar. Stir over a moderate heat until thickened and smooth. Remove from the heat.

2 Grate a few long shreds of orange rind from the orange and save for decoration. Finely grate the remaining rind. Cut all the peel and white pith from the orange and remove the segments. Stir into the semolina with the orange rind.

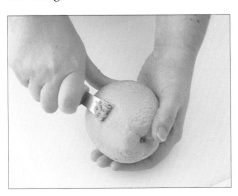

3 Whisk the egg white until stiff but not dry, then fold lightly and evenly into the mixture. Spoon into a 4 cup ovenproof dish and bake for 15–20 minutes, until puffed and golden brown. Serve immediately.

COOK'S TIP
When using the rind of citrus fruit, scrub the fruit thoroughly before use, or buy unwaxed fruit.

NUTRITION NOTES

Per portion:
Energy	158Kcals/665kJ
Fat	2.67g
Saturated fat	1.54g
Cholesterol	10.5mg
Fiber	0.86g

Banana Maple, and Lime Crêpes

Crêpes are a treat any day of the week, and they can be made in advance and stored in the freezer for convenience.

INGREDIENTS

Serves 4
1 cup flour
1 egg white
1 cup skim milk
¼ cup cold water
sunflower oil, for frying

For the filling
4 bananas, sliced
3 tbsp maple syrup
2 tbsp lime juice
strips of lime rind, to decorate

1 Beat together the flour, egg white, milk, and water until smooth and bubbly. Chill until needed.

2 Heat a small amount of oil in a nonstick frying pan and pour in enough batter just to coat the base. Swirl it around the pan to coat evenly.

3 Cook until golden, then toss or turn and cook the other side. Place on a plate, cover with foil, and keep hot while making the remaining crêpes.

4 To make the filling, place the bananas, syrup, and lime juice in a pan and simmer gently for 1 minute. Spoon into the crêpes and fold into quarters. Sprinkle with shreds of lime rind to decorate. Serve hot, with yogurt or low fat fromage frais.

COOK'S TIP
Crêpes freeze well. To store for later use, interleave them with nonstick baking paper, wrap, and freeze for up to 3 months.

NUTRITION NOTES

Per portion:
Energy	282Kcals/1185kJ
Fat	2.79g
Saturated fat	0.47g
Cholesterol	1.25mg
Fiber	2.12g

SPICED PEARS IN CIDER

Any variety of pear can be used for cooking, but it is best to choose firm pears for this recipe, or they will break up easily – Bosc are a good choice.

INGREDIENTS

Serves 4
4 medium firm pears
1 cup dry cider
thinly pared strip of lemon rind
1 cinnamon stick
2 tbsp brown sugar
1 tsp arrowroot
ground cinnamon, to sprinkle

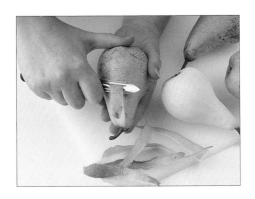

1 Peel the pears thinly, leaving them whole with the stems on. Place in a pan with the cider, lemon rind, and cinnamon. Cover and simmer gently, turning the pears occasionally for 15–20 minutes, or until tender.

2 Lift out the pears. Boil the syrup, uncovered, to reduce by about half. Remove the lemon rind and cinnamon stick, then stir in the sugar.

3 Mix the arrowroot with 1 tbsp cold water in a small bowl until smooth, then stir into the syrup. Bring to a boil and stir over the heat until thickened and clear.

4 Pour the sauce over the pears and sprinkle with ground cinnamon. Leave to cool slightly, then serve warm with low fat fromage frais.

COOK'S TIP
Whole pears look very impressive, but if you prefer, they can be halved and cored before cooking. This will reduce the cooking time slightly.

NUTRITION NOTES

Per portion:
Energy	102Kcals/428kJ
Fat	0.18g
Saturated fat	0.01g
Cholesterol	0
Fiber	1.65g

COLD DESSERTS

From fresh, colorful fruit salads to refreshing, tangy sorbets, healthy cold desserts should be the easiest part of selecting dishes for your low fat menus. The year-round huge variety of fresh fruit gives a head start – even the simplest platter of fresh fruits can make an exotic dessert. Time was when ice creams, mousses, and cheesecakes were without exception rich, elaborate and high in fat, certainly to be avoided in excess. But the rapidly expanding range of low fat dairy products such as fromage frais, yogurt, and crème fraîche, means that lighter, far less rich versions are now possible. So, if plain fresh fruit is just not enough, you can tuck into a luscious scoop of Banana Honey Yogurt Ice or a slice of Creamy Mango Cheesecake without a trace of guilt.

FLUFFY BANANA AND PINEAPPLE MOUSSE

This light mousse looks really impressive but is remarkably easy to make, especially with a food processor or blender. You could try substituting the canned pineapple chunks for other canned fruits such as peach or apricot slices.

INGREDIENTS

Serves 6
2 ripe bananas
1 cup cottage cheese
15oz can pineapple chunks or pieces in juice
1 sachet powdered gelatin
2 egg whites

NUTRITION NOTES

Per portion:	
Energy	110Kcals/464kJ
Fat	1.6g
Saturated fat	0.98g
Cholesterol	4.88mg
Fiber	0.51g

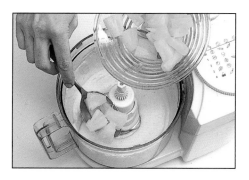

1 Tie a double band of nonstick parchment paper around the outside of a 2½ cup soufflé dish, to come 2in above the rim.

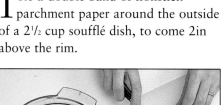

2 Peel and chop one banana and place it in a food processor or blender with the cottage cheese. Process until smooth.

3 Drain the pineapple, reserving the juice, and reserve a few pieces or chunks for decoration. Add the rest to the banana mixture and process for a few seconds until finely chopped. Transfer the mixture to a large bowl.

4 In a small bowl, add the gelatin to 4 tbsp of the reserved pineapple juice. Heat over hot water to dissolve, then stir quickly into the fruit mixture.

5 In a separate bowl, quickly whisk the egg whites until they hold soft peaks, then fold them lightly and evenly into the fruit mixture. Tip the mousse into the prepared dish, smooth the surface and chill until set.

6 When the mousse is set, carefully remove the paper collar. Decorate the mousse with the reserved banana and pineapple.

> **COOK'S TIP**
> For a simpler way of serving, use a 4 cup serving dish, but do not tie a collar around the edge.

ROSE-SCENTED FRUIT COMPOTE

Rose-scented tea gives this dessert a lovely subtle flavor.

INGREDIENTS

Serves 4

1 tsp rose pouchong tea
1 tsp rose water (optional)
¼ cup sugar
1 tsp lemon juice
5 dessert apples
1½ cups raspberries, thawed,
   if frozen

NUTRITION NOTES

Per portion:

Energy	141Kcals/591kJ
Fat	0.34g
Saturated fat	0
Cholesterol	0
Fiber	3.94g

1 Warm a large teapot. Add the rose pouchong tea and 3¾ cups of boiling water together with the rose water, if using. Allow to stand and infuse for about 4 minutes.

2 Measure the sugar and lemon juice into a stainless steel saucepan. Strain in the tea and stir to dissolve the sugar.

3 Peel and quarter the apples, then remove the cores.

4 Add the apples to the syrup and poach for about 5 minutes.

5 Transfer the apples and syrup to a large metal tray and leave to cool to room temperature.

6 Pour the cooled apples and syrup into a bowl, add the raspberries and mix to combine. Spoon into individual glass dishes or bowls and serve.

COOK'S TIP

If fresh raspberries are out of season, use the same weight of frozen fruit or a 14oz can of well-drained fruit.

Creamy Mango Cheesecake

Cheesecakes are always a favorite but sadly they are often high in fat. This one is the exception.

Ingredients

Serves 4

1¼ cups oatmeal
3 tbsp sunflower margarine
2 tbsp clear honey
1 large ripe mango
1¼ cups low fat cream cheese
⅔ cup low fat plain yogurt
finely grated rind of 1 small lime
3 tbsp apple juice
4 tsp powdered gelatin
fresh mango and lime slices, to decorate

1 Preheat the oven to 400°F. Mix together the oatmeal, margarine, and honey. Press the mixture into the base of a 8in loose-bottomed cake pan. Bake for 12–15 minutes, until lightly browned. Cool.

2 Peel, pit, and roughly chop the mango. Place the chopped mango, cheese, yogurt, and lime rind in a food processor and process until smooth.

3 Heat the apple juice until boiling, sprinkle the gelatin over it, stir to dissolve, then stir into cheese mixture.

4 Pour the cheese mixture into the pan and chill until set, then turn out onto a serving plate. Decorate the top with mango and lime slices.

Nutrition Notes

Per portion:

Energy	422Kcals/1774kJ
Fat	11.37g
Saturated fat	2.2g
Cholesterol	2.95mg
Fiber	7.15g

Frudités with Honey Dip

Ingredients

Serves 4

1 cup thick, plain, yogurt
3 tbsp clear honey
selection of fresh fruit for dipping such as apples, pears, tangerines, grapes, figs, cherries, strawberries, and kiwi fruit

Nutrition Notes

Per portion:

Energy	161Kcals/678kJ
Fat	5.43g
Saturated fat	3.21g
Cholesterol	7.31mg
Fiber	2.48g

1 Place the yogurt in a dish, beat until smooth, then stir in the honey, leaving a little marbled effect.

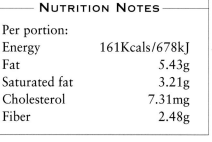

2 Cut the fruits into wedges or bite-sized pieces, or leave whole.

3 Arrange the fruits on a platter with the bowl of dip in the center. Serve chilled.

YOGURT RING WITH TROPICAL FRUIT

Serves 6
¾ cup tropical fruit juice
1 sachet powdered gelatin
3 egg whites
⅔ cup plain low fat yogurt
finely grated rind of 1 lime

For the filling
1 mango
2 kiwi fruit
10–12 cape gooseberries
juice of 1 lime

Per portion:	
Energy	98Kcals/410kJ
Fat	0.57g
Saturated fat	0.13g
Cholesterol	1mg
Fiber	2.72g

1 Place the fruit juice in a saucepan and sprinkle the gelatin over. Heat gently until the gelatin has dissolved.

2 Whisk the egg whites in a clean, dry bowl until they hold soft peaks. Continue whisking hard, while gradually adding the yogurt and lime rind.

3 Continue whisking hard and pour in the hot gelatin mixture.

4 Mix the gelatin mixture until everything is combined. Quickly pour the mixture into a 6¼ cup ring mould. Chill the mould in the fridge until set. The mixture will separate into two layers.

5 For the filling, halve, pit, peel and dice the mango. Peel and slice the kiwi fruit. Remove the outer leaves from the cape gooseberries and cut in half. Toss all the fruits together and stir in the lime juice.

6 Run a knife around the edge of the ring to loosen the mixture. Dip the mould quickly into cold water and then turn it out on to a serving plate. Spoon all the prepared fruit into the center of the ring and serve immediately.

SUMMER FRUIT SALAD ICE CREAM

This beautiful ice cream contains delicious mixed summer fruits.

INGREDIENTS

Serves 6

8 cups mixed soft summer fruit, such as raspberries, strawberries, black currants and red currants
2 eggs, separated
1 cup plain low fat strained yogurt
¾ cup red grape juice
1 sachet powdered gelatin

NUTRITION NOTES

Per portion:

Energy	133Kcals/558kJ
Fat	5.69g
Saturated fat	2.72g
Cholesterol	78.02mg
Fiber	3.6g

1 Reserve half the fruit and purée the rest in a food processor or blender, or rub it through a strainer to make a smooth purée.

2 Whisk the egg yolks and yogurt into the fruit purée.

3 Heat the grape juice until almost boiling. Remove from the heat, sprinkle the gelatin over the juice and stir to dissolve the gelatin completely.

4 Whisk the dissolved gelatin into the fruit purée. Pour into a freezer container. Freeze until slushy.

5 Whisk the egg whites until they are stiff. Quickly fold them into the half-frozen mixture.

6 Return to the freezer and freeze until almost firm. Scoop into individual dishes or glasses and decorate with the reserved soft fruits.

COOK'S TIP
Red grape juice has a good flavor and improves the color of the ice, but if it is not available, you can use cranberry, apple or orange juice instead.

GRAPE CHEESE WHIP

INGREDIENTS

Serves 4

1 cup purple or green seedless grapes,
* plus 4 sprigs*
2 egg whites
1 tbsp sugar
finely grated rind and juice of ½ lemon
1 cup low fat cream cheese
3 tbsp clear honey
2 tbsp brandy (optional)

NUTRITION NOTES

Per portion:

Energy	135Kcals/563kJ
Fat	0
Saturated fat	0
Cholesterol	0.56mg
Fiber	0

1 Brush the sprigs of grapes lightly with egg white and sprinkle with sugar to coat. Leave to dry.

2 Mix together the lemon rind and juice, cheese, honey, and brandy. Chop the remaining grapes and stir in.

3 Whisk the egg whites until stiff enough to hold soft peaks. Fold the whites into the grape mixture, then spoon into serving glasses.

4 Top with sugar-frosted grapes and serve chilled.

STRAWBERRIES IN SPICED GRAPE JELLY

INGREDIENTS

Serves 4

1⅞ cups red grape juice
1 cinnamon stick
1 small orange
1 envelope gelatin
2 cups strawberries, chopped
strawberries and orange rind, to
* decorate*

1 Place the grape juice in a pan with the cinnamon. Thinly pare the rind from the orange and add to the pan. Infuse over a very low heat for 10 minutes, then remove the flavorings.

2 Squeeze the juice from the orange and sprinkle over the gelatin. Stir into the grape juice to dissolve. Allow to cool until just beginning to set.

3 Stir in the strawberries and quickly tip into a 4 cup mold or serving dish. Chill until set.

4 To turn out, dip the mold quickly into hot water and invert onto a serving plate. Decorate with fresh strawberries and shreds of orange rind.

NUTRITION NOTES

Per portion:

Energy	85Kcals/355kJ
Fat	0.2g
Saturated fat	0
Cholesterol	0
Fiber	1.04g

PEARS IN MAPLE AND YOGURT SAUCE

INGREDIENTS

Serves 6

6 firm pears
1 tbsp lemon juice
1 cup sweet white wine or
   sweet cider
thinly pared rind of 1 lemon
1 cinnamon stick
2 tbsp maple syrup
½ tsp arrowroot
⅔ cup plain low fat
   strained yogurt

NUTRITION NOTES

Per portion:
Energy	132Kcals/556kJ
Fat	2.4g
Saturated fat	1.43g
Cholesterol	3.25mg
Fiber	2.64g

1 Thinly peel the pears, leaving them whole and with stalks intact. Brush them with lemon juice, to prevent them from browning. Use a potato peeler or small knife to scoop out the core from the base of each pear.

2 Place the pears in a wide, heavy saucepan and pour over the wine or cider, with enough cold water almost to cover the pears.

3 Add the lemon rind and cinnamon stick, and then bring to a boil. Reduce the heat, and simmer the pears gently for 30–40 minutes, or until tender. Turn the pears occasionally. Lift the pears out carefully, draining them well, and set aside.

4 Bring the pear cooking liquid to a boil and boil uncovered to reduce to about ½ cup.

5 Strain the liquid and add the maple syrup. Blend a little of the liquid with the arrowroot. Return to the pan and cook, stirring, until thick and clear. Leave to cool.

6 Slice each pear about three-quarters of the way through, leaving the slices attached at the stem end. Fan each pear out on a serving plate.

7 Stir 2 tbsp of the cooled syrup into the yogurt and spoon it around the pears. Drizzle with the remaining syrup and serve immediately.

COOK'S TIP
Poach the pears in advance, and have the cooled syrup ready to spoon on to the plates just before serving. The cooking time of this dish will vary, depending upon the type and ripeness of the pears. The pears should be ripe, but still firm – over-ripe ones will not keep their shape well.

ICED APPLE AND BLACKBERRY TERRINE

Apples and blackberries are a classic combination for fall; they really complement each other. This pretty, three-layered terrine is frozen, so you can enjoy it at any time of year.

--- INGREDIENTS ---

Serves 6

1lb cooking or eating apples
1¼ cups sweet cider
1 tbsp clear honey
1 tsp vanilla essence
2 cups fresh or frozen and thawed
*   blackberries*
1 sachet powdered gelatin
2 egg whites
fresh apple slices and blackberries,
*   to decorate*

--- NUTRITION NOTES ---

Per portion:
Energy	78Kcals/328kJ
Fat	0.18g
Saturated fat	0
Cholesterol	0
Fiber	2.37g

3 Heat the remaining cider until almost boiling, then sprinkle the gelatin over and stir until the gelatin has completely dissolved. Add half the gelatin to the apple purée and half to the blackberry purée.

4 Leave the apple and blackberry purées to cool until almost set. Whisk the egg whites until they are stiff. Quickly fold them into the apple purée. Remove half the purée to another bowl. Stir the remaining whole blackberries into half the apple purée, and then tip this into a 7½ cup loaf pan, packing it down firmly.

5 Top with the blackberry purée and spread it evenly. Finally, add a layer of the apple purée and smooth it evenly. (If necessary, freeze each layer until firm before adding the next.)

6 Freeze until firm. To serve, allow to stand at room temperature for 20 minutes to soften, then place slices, decorated with fresh apple slices and blackberries, on individual plates.

COOK'S TIP
To set without layering, purée the apples and blackberries together, stir in the dissolved gelatin and whisked egg whites, turn into the pan and leave to set.

1 Peel, core and chop the apples, and place them in a saucepan with half the cider. Bring to a boil, then cover the pan and simmer gently until tender.

2 Tip the apples into a food processor or blender and process to a smooth purée. Stir in the honey and vanilla. Add half the blackberries to half the apple purée, and process again until smooth. Strain to remove the seeds.

FRESH CITRUS JELLY

Fresh fruit jellies really are worth the effort – they make a stunning fat-free dessert and are also rich in vitamins.

INGREDIENTS

Serves 4
3 oranges
1 lemon
1 lime
1¼ cups water
⅓ cup golden superfine sugar
1 sachet powdered gelatin
extra slices of fruit, to decorate

NUTRITION NOTES

Per portion:

Energy	136Kcals/573kJ
Fat	0.21g
Saturated fat	0
Cholesterol	0
Fiber	2.13g

1 With a sharp knife, cut all the peel and white pith from one orange and carefully remove the segments. Arrange all of the segments in the base of a 3¾ cup mould or dish.

2 Remove some shreds of citrus rind with a zester and reserve them for decoration. Grate the remaining rind from the lemon and lime and one orange. Place all the grated rind in a saucepan with the water and sugar.

3 Heat gently until the sugar has dissolved. Remove from the heat. Squeeze the juice from all the rest of the fruit and stir it into the pan.

4 Strain the liquid into a measuring cup to remove the rind (you should have about 2½ cups: if necessary, make up the amount with water). Sprinkle the gelatin over the liquid and stir until dissolved.

5 Pour a little of the jelly over the orange segments and chill until it has set. Leave the remaining jelly at room temperature to cool, but do not allow it to set.

6 Pour the remaining cooled jelly into the dish and chill until set. To serve, turn out the jelly and decorate it with the reserved citrus rind shreds and slices of citrus fruit.

> **COOK'S TIP**
> To speed up the setting of the fruit segments in jelly, stand the dish in a bowl of ice.

SPICED PINEAPPLE WEDGES WITH LIME

Fresh pineapple is easy to prepare and always looks very festive, so this dish is perfect for easy entertaining.

INGREDIENTS

Serves 4
1 ripe pineapple
1 lime
1 tbsp dark brown sugar
1 tsp ground allspice

NUTRITION NOTES

Per portion:
Energy	71Kcals/296kJ
Fat	0.39 g
Saturated fat	0.03g
Cholesterol	0
Fiber	1.5g

COOK'S TIP
For a quick hot dish, place the pineapple slices on a baking sheet, sprinkle with the lime juice, sugar and allspice, and place them under a hot broiler for 3–4 minutes, or until golden and bubbling. Sprinkle with shreds of lime zest and serve.

1 Cut the pineapple lengthwise into quarters and remove the core. Make sure you use a sharp knife and hold the pineapple firmly.

2 Loosen the flesh with a sharp knife. Cut the flesh into slices, leaving it on the skin.

3 Remove some shreds of rind from the lime and squeeze.

4 Sprinkle the pineapple with the lime juice and zest, sugar and allspice. Serve immediately, or for better results chill for up to an hour.

COOK'S TIP
When buying a fresh pineapple, choose a fruit with stiff leaves. Pineapples can be used to make a variety of desserts, and their shells make attractive containers for fruit salads, pineapple sorbet and ice creams.

EMERALD FRUIT SALAD

INGREDIENTS

Serves 4
2 tbsp lime juice
2 tbsp clear honey
2 green eating apples, cored and sliced
1 small ripe melon, diced
2 kiwi fruit, sliced
1 star fruit, sliced
mint sprigs, to decorate

1 Mix together the lime juice and honey in a large bowl, then toss the apple slices in this.

2 Stir in the melon, kiwi fruit and star fruit. Place in a glass serving dish and chill before serving.

3 Decorate with mint sprigs and serve with yogurt or fromage frais.

> **COOK'S TIP**
> Star fruit is best when fully ripe – look for plump, yellow fruit.

NUTRITION NOTES

Per portion:

Energy	93Kcals/390kJ
Fat	0.48g
Saturated fat	0
Cholesterol	0
Fiber	2.86g

PEACH AND GINGER PASHKA

This simpler adaptation of a Russian Easter favorite is made with much lighter ingredients than the traditional version.

INGREDIENTS

Serves 4–6
1½ cups low fat cottage cheese
2 ripe peaches or nectarines
⅓ cup low fat plain yogurt
2 pieces preserved ginger in syrup, drained and chopped
2 tbsp ginger syrup
½ tsp vanilla extract
peach slices and toasted slivered almonds, to decorate

NUTRITION NOTES

Per portion:

Energy	142Kcals/600kJ
Fat	1.63g
Saturated fat	0.22g
Cholesterol	1.77mg
Fiber	1.06g

1 Drain the cottage cheese and press through a strainer into a bowl. Pit and roughly chop the peaches.

2 Mix together the chopped peaches, cottage cheese, yogurt, ginger, syrup, and vanilla extract.

3 Line a new, clean flower pot or a strainer with a piece of clean, fine cloth such as cheesecloth.

4 Tip in the cheese mixture, then wrap over the cloth and place a weight on top. Leave over a bowl in a cool place to drain overnight. To serve, unwrap the cloth and invert the pashka on to a plate. Decorate with peach slices and almonds.

PLUM AND PORT SORBET

This is more of a sorbet for grown-ups, but you could use red grape juice in place of the port if you prefer.

INGREDIENTS

Serves 4–6
2 lb ripe red plums, halved and pitted
6 tbsp sugar
3 tbsp water
3 tbsp ruby port or red wine
plain cookies, to serve

1 Place the plums in a pan with the sugar and water. Stir over gentle heat until the sugar is melted, then cover and simmer gently for about 5 minutes, until the fruit is soft.

2 Turn into a food processor and purée until smooth, then stir in the port. Cool completely, then tip into a freezer container and freeze until firm around the edges.

3 Spoon into the food processor and process until smooth. Return to the freezer and freeze until solid.

4 Allow to soften slightly at room temperature for 15–20 minutes before serving in scoops, with plain cookies.

NUTRITION NOTES

Per portion:

Energy	166Kcals/699kJ
Fat	0.25g
Saturated fat	0
Cholesterol	0
Fiber	3.75g

TOFU BERRY BRULÉE

This is a lighter variation of a classic dessert, usually forbidden on a low fat diet, using tofu, which is low in fat and free from cholesterol. Use any soft berry fruits in season.

INGREDIENTS

Serves 4

11oz packet tofu
3 tbsp confectioners' sugar
1½ cups red berries, such as raspberries, strawberries, and red currants
about 5 tbsp raw sugar

1 Place the tofu and confectioners' sugar in a food processor or blender and process until smooth.

2 Stir in the fruits and spoon into a 3¾ cup flameproof dish. Sprinkle the top with enough raw sugar to cover evenly.

3 Place under a very hot broiler until the sugar melts and caramelizes. Chill before serving.

COOK'S TIP
Choose smooth tofu rather than firm tofu as it gives a better texture in this type of dish. Firm tofu is better for cooking in chunks.

NUTRITION NOTES

Per portion:	
Energy	180Kcals/760kJ
Fat	3.01g
Saturated fat	0.41g
Cholesterol	0
Fiber	1.31g

Apricot Mousse

This light, fluffy dessert can be made with any dried fruits instead of apricots – try dried peaches, prunes, or apples.

─── **Ingredients** ───

Serves 4
1½ cups dried apricots
1¼ cups fresh orange juice
⅞ cup low fat fromage frais
2 egg whites
mint sprigs, to decorate

1 Place the apricots in a saucepan with the orange juice and heat gently until boiling. Cover the pan and simmer gently for 3 minutes.

2 Cool slightly. Place in a food processor or blender and process until smooth. Stir in the fromage frais.

3 Whisk the egg whites until stiff enough to hold soft peaks, then fold into the apricot mixture.

4 Spoon into four stemmed glasses or one large serving dish. Chill before serving.

┌─────────────────────────────┐
COOK'S TIP
For an even quicker version, omit the egg whites and simply swirl together the apricot mixture and fromage frais.
└─────────────────────────────┘

─── **Nutrition Notes** ───

Per portion:	
Energy	180Kcals/757kJ
Fat	0.63g
Saturated fat	0.06g
Cholesterol	0.5mg
Fiber	4.8g

APPLE FOAM WITH BLACKBERRIES

Any seasonal berry can be used for this if blackberries are not available.

INGREDIENTS

Serves 4
2 cups blackberries
⅔ cup apple juice
1 tsp powdered gelatin
1 tbsp clear honey
2 egg whites

1 Place the blackberries in a pan with 4 tbsp of the apple juice and heat gently until the fruit is soft. Remove from the heat, cool, and chill.

2 Sprinkle the gelatin over the remaining apple juice in a small pan and stir over low heat until dissolved. Stir in the honey.

3 Whisk the egg whites until they hold stiff peaks. Continue whisking hard and pour in the hot gelatin mixture gradually, until well mixed.

4 Quickly spoon the foam into rough mounds on individual plates. Chill. Serve with the blackberries and juice spooned around.

COOK'S TIP
Make sure that you dissolve the gelatin over very low heat. It must not boil, or it will lose its setting ability.

NUTRITION NOTES

Per portion:
Energy	49Kcals/206kJ
Fat	0.15g
Saturated fat	0
Cholesterol	0
Fiber	1.74g

BANANA-HONEY YOGURT ICE

INGREDIENTS

Serves 4–6

4 ripe bananas, chopped coarsely
1 tbsp lemon juice
2 tbsp clear honey
1 cup thick, plain yogurt
½ tsp ground cinnamon
plain cookies, slivered hazelnuts, and
banana slices, to serve

NUTRITION NOTES

Per portion:
Energy	138Kcals/580kJ
Fat	7.37g
Saturated fat	3.72g
Cholesterol	8.13mg
Fiber	0.47g

1 Place the bananas in a food processor or blender with the lemon juice, honey, yogurt, and cinnamon. Process until smooth and creamy.

2 Pour the mixture into a freezer container and freeze until almost solid. Spoon back into the food processor and process again until smooth.

3 Return to the freezer until firm. Allow to soften at room temperature for 15 minutes, then serve in scoops, with plain cookies, slivered hazelnuts, and banana slices.

AUTUMN PUDDING

INGREDIENTS

Serves 6

10 slices white or whole-wheat bread,
    at least 1 day old
1 tart cooking apple, peeled, cored, and
    sliced
8oz ripe red plums, halved and pitted
8oz blackberries
4 tbsp water
6 tbsp sugar

1 Remove the crusts from the bread and use a cookie cutter to stamp out a 3in round from one slice. Cut the remaining slices in half.

2 Place the bread round in the base of a 5 cup pudding bowl, then overlap the fingers around the sides, saving some for the top.

3 Place the apple, plums, blackberries, water, and sugar in a pan, heat gently until the sugar dissolves, then simmer gently for 10 minutes, or until soft. Remove from the heat.

4 Reserve the juice and spoon the fruit into the bread-lined bowl. Top with the reserved bread, then spoon over the reserved fruit juices.

5 Cover the mold with a saucer and place weights on top. Chill the pudding overnight. Turn out onto a serving plate and serve with low fat yogurt or fromage frais.

NUTRITION NOTES

Per portion:
Energy	197Kcals/830kJ
Fat	1.1g
Saturated fat	0.2g
Cholesterol	0
Fiber	2.84g

FRUITED RICE RING

This unusual rice pudding looks beautiful turned out of a ring mold but if you prefer, stir the fruit into the rice and serve in individual dishes.

INGREDIENTS

Serves 4
5 tbsp short-grain rice
3¾ cups low fat milk
1 cinnamon stick
1½ cups mixed dried fruit
¾ cup orange juice
3 tbsp sugar
finely grated rind of 1 small orange

1 Place the rice, milk, and cinnamon stick in a large pan and bring to a boil. Cover and simmer, stirring occasionally, for about 1½ hours, until no liquid remains.

2 Meanwhile, place the fruit and orange juice in another pan and bring to a boil. Cover and simmer very gently for about 1 hour, until tender and no liquid remains.

3 Remove the cinnamon stick from the rice and stir in the sugar and orange rind.

4 Tip the fruit into the base of a lightly oiled 6 cup ring mold. Spoon the rice over, smoothing down firmly. Chill.

5 Run a knife around the edge of the mold and turn out the rice carefully on to a serving plate.

NUTRITION NOTES

Per portion:
Energy	343Kcals/1440kJ
Fat	4.4g
Saturated fat	2.26g
Cholesterol	15.75mg
Fiber	1.07g

RASPBERRY-PASSIONFRUIT SWIRLS

If passionfruit is not available, this simple dessert can be made with raspberries alone.

INGREDIENTS

Serves 4
2½ cups raspberries
2 passionfruit
1⅔ cups low fat fromage frais
2 tbsp sugar
raspberries and sprigs of mint, to decorate

1 Mash the raspberries in a small bowl with a fork until the juice runs. Scoop out the passionfruit pulp into a separate bowl with the fromage frais and sugar and mix well.

2 Spoon alternate spoonfuls of the raspberry pulp and the fromage frais mixture into stemmed glasses or one large serving dish, stirring lightly to create a swirled effect.

3 Decorate each dessert with a whole raspberry and a sprig of fresh mint. Serve chilled.

COOK'S TIP
Over-ripe, slightly soft fruit can also be used in this recipe. Use frozen raspberries when fresh are not available, but thaw first.

NUTRITION NOTES

Per portion:

Energy	110Kcals/462kJ
Fat	0.47g
Saturated fat	0.13g
Cholesterol	1mg
Fiber	2.12g

RED BERRY SPONGE TART

When soft berry fruits are in season, try making this delicious sponge tart. Serve warm from the oven with scoops of low fat vanilla ice cream, if you wish.

INGREDIENTS

Serves 4
softened low fat margarine,
    for greasing
4 cups soft berry fruits such as
    raspberries, blackberries, black
    currants, red currants, strawberries
    or blueberries
2 eggs, at room temperature
¼ cup superfine sugar, plus extra to
    taste (optional)
1 tbsp flour
¼ cup ground almonds
low fat vanilla ice cream, to
    serve (optional)

NUTRITION NOTES

Per portion:
Energy	219Kcals/919kJ
Fat	11.31g
Saturated fat	2.05g
Cholesterol	112.6mg
Fiber	4.49g

COOK'S TIP
When berry fruits are out of season, use bottled fruits, but make sure that they are very well drained before use.

1 Preheat the oven to 375°F. Brush a 9in quiche pan with low fat margarine and line the bottom with a circle of nonstick parchment paper. Scatter the fruit in the base of the pan with a little sugar if the fruits are tart.

2 Whisk the eggs and sugar together for about 3–4 minutes or until they leave a thick trail across the surface. Combine the flour and almonds, then fold into the egg mixture with a spatula – retaining as much air as possible.

3 Spread the mixture on top of the fruit base and bake in the preheated oven for about 15 minutes. Turn out on to a serving plate and serve, with low fat vanilla ice cream if you like.

COOK'S TIP
Fresh soft berry fruits are best used on the day of purchase. If you purchase them in traditional punnets, avoid any badly stained containers.

RASPBERRY PASSIONFRUIT PUFFS

Few desserts are so strikingly easy to make as this one: beaten egg whites and sugar baked in a dish, turned out and served with a handful of soft fruit and ready-made custard from a carton.

INGREDIENTS

Serves 4

2 tbsp low fat margarine, softened
5 egg whites
²⁄₃ cup superfine sugar
2 passionfruit
6 cups fresh raspberries
1 cup low fat ready-made custard from a carton or can
skim milk, as required
confectioner's sugar, for dusting

NUTRITION NOTES

Per portion:

Energy	309Kcals/1296kJ
Fat	5.74g
Saturated fat	3.3g
Cholesterol	15.81mg
Fiber	4.47g

1 Preheat the oven to 350°F. With a brush, paint four 1¼ cup ovenproof soufflé dishes with a visible layer of low fat margarine.

2 Whisk the egg whites in a mixing bowl until firm. (You can use an electric mixer.) Add the sugar a little at a time and whisk into a firm meringue.

3 Halve the passionfruit, take out the seeds with a spoon and fold them into the meringue.

4 Turn the meringue out into the four prepared dishes, stand in a deep roasting pan which has been half-filled with boiling water and bake for about 10 minutes.

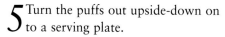

5 Turn the puffs out upside-down on to a serving plate.

6 Top the puffs with the fresh raspberries. Thin the custard with a little skim milk and pour around the edge. Dredge with confectioner's sugar and serve warm or cold.

COOK'S TIP

If raspberries are out of season, use either fresh, bottled or canned soft fruit such as strawberries, blueberries or red currants.

CAKES, BAKES AND BREADS

The main advantage of baking your own cakes and cookies is that you can control exactly what goes into them. Most commercially produced cakes and bakes contain a high proportion of saturated fats, but it is possible to bake at home using less fat, different types of fat, and often less sugar too. All the bakes in this chapter are low in fat, and in many cases contain little or no eggs, and often sugar is reduced by using fruits to sweeten the mixture. The main drawback is that the cakes will not keep for nearly as long as traditional recipes, but it is a problem far outweighed by the health advantages. So, as you fill the cookie jar with Apricot Yogurt Cookies or serve up that luscious slice of Carrot Cake, your conscience is clear – let them eat cake!

SPIRAL HERB BREAD

An attractive and delicious bread which is ideal for serving with a salad for a healthy lunch.

INGREDIENTS

Makes 2 loaves
2 tbsp fast-rising dried yeast
2½ cups lukewarm water
3⅔ cups white bread flour
3½ cups whole-wheat flour
3 tsp salt
2 tbsp sunflower margarine
1 large bunch parsley, finely chopped
1 bunch scallions, chopped
1 garlic clove, finely chopped
salt and black pepper
1 egg, lightly beaten
skim milk, for glazing

NUTRITION NOTES

Per loaf:
Energy	1698Kcals/7132kJ
Fat	24.55g
Saturated fat	9.87g
Cholesterol	144.33mg
Fiber	30.96g

1 Mix together the yeast with about ¼ cup of the water, stir and leave to dissolve.

2 Mix together the flours and salt in a large bowl. Make a well in the center and pour in the yeast mixture and the remaining water. With a wooden spoon, stir from the center, working outwards to obtain a rough dough.

3 Transfer the dough to a floured surface and knead until smooth and elastic. Return to the bowl, cover with a plastic bag, and leave until doubled in volume, about 2 hours.

4 Meanwhile, combine the margarine, parsley, scallions and garlic in a large frying pan. Cook over a low heat, stirring, until softened. Season and set aside.

5 Grease two 9 x 5in loaf pans. When the dough has risen, cut in half and roll each half into a rectangle about 14 x 9in.

6 Brush both with the beaten egg. Divide the herb mixture between the two, spreading just up to the edges.

7 Roll up to enclose the filling and pinch the short ends to seal. Place in the pans, seam-side down.

8 Cover the dough with a clean dish towel and leave undisturbed in a warm place until the dough rises above the rim of the pans.

9 Preheat the oven to 375°F. Brush the loaves with milk and bake until the bottoms sound hollow when tapped, about 55 minutes. Cool on a wire rack.

WALNUT BREAD

Delicious at any time of day, this bread may be eaten plain or topped with some low fat cream cheese or margarine.

INGREDIENTS

Makes 1 loaf

2½ cups whole-wheat flour
1¼ cups white bread flour
2½ tsp salt
2¼ cups lukewarm water
1 tbsp clear honey
1 tbsp fast-rising dried yeast
1¼ cups walnut pieces, plus more for decorating
1 egg, beaten, for glazing

NUTRITION NOTES

Per loaf:
Energy	2852Kcals/11980kJ
Fat	109.34g
Saturated fat	12.04g
Cholesterol	77mg
Fiber	47.04g

1 Mix together the flours and salt in a large bowl. Make a well in the center and pour in 1 cup of the water, the honey and the yeast.

2 Set aside until the yeast dissolves and the mixture is bubbly.

3 Add the remaining water. With a wooden spoon, stir from the center, incorporating flour with each turn, to obtain a smooth dough. Add more flour if the dough is too sticky and use your hands if the dough becomes too stiff to stir.

4 Transfer to a floured board and knead, adding flour if necessary, until the dough is smooth and elastic. Place in a greased bowl and roll the dough around in the bowl to coat thoroughly all over.

5 Cover with a plastic bag and leave in a warm place until doubled in volume, about 1½ hours.

6 Punch down the dough very firmly and knead in the walnuts until they are evenly distributed.

7 Grease a cookie sheet. Shape the dough into a round loaf and place on the sheet. Press in the walnut pieces to decorate the top. Cover loosely with a damp dish towel and leave to rise in a warm place until doubled in size for about 25–30 minutes.

8 Preheat the oven to 425°F. With a sharp knife, score the top of the loaf and brush with the egg glaze. Bake for 15 minutes. Lower the temperature to 375°F and bake until the bottom sounds hollow when tapped, about 40 minutes. Leave to cool.

OATMEAL BREAD

A healthy bread, with a delightfully crumbly texture due to the inclusion of rolled oats.

INGREDIENTS

Makes 2 loaves
2 *cups skim milk*
2 *tbsp low fat margarine*
1¼ *cups dark brown sugar*
2 *tsp salt*
1 *tbsp fast-rising dried yeast*
¼ *cup lukewarm water*
3½ *cups rolled oats*
4–6 *cups white bread flour*

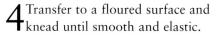

1 Scald the milk. Remove from the heat and stir in the margarine, sugar and salt. Leave until lukewarm.

2 Combine the yeast and lukewarm water in a large bowl and leave until the yeast is dissolved and the mixture is bubbly. Stir in the milk mixture.

3 Add 2½ cups of the rolled oats and enough of the flour to obtain a soft pliable dough.

4 Transfer to a floured surface and knead until smooth and elastic.

5 Place the dough in a greased bowl, cover with a plastic bag, and leave it until doubled in volume for about 2–3 hours. Grease a large cookie sheet.

6 Transfer the dough to a lightly floured surface and divide in half.

7 Shape into rounds. Place on the cookie sheet, cover with a damp dish towel and leave to rise until doubled in volume, about 1 hour.

8 Preheat the oven to 400°F. Score the tops of the loaves and sprinkle with the remaining oats. Bake until the bottoms sound hollow when tapped, about 45–50 minutes. Transfer to wire racks and leave to cool.

NUTRITION NOTES	
Per loaf:	
Energy	2281Kcals/9581kJ
Fat	34.46g
Saturated fat	11.94g
Cholesterol	39mg
Fiber	24.11g

APRICOT AND ORANGE ROULADE

This elegant dessert is very good served with a spoonful or two of plain yogurt.

INGREDIENTS

Serves 6

4 egg whites
½ cup golden superfine sugar
½ cup flour
finely grated rind of 1 small orange
3 tbsp orange juice
2 tsp confectioner's sugar and shreds of orange zest, to decorate

For the filling
⅔ cup ready-to-eat dried apricots
⅔ cup orange juice

NUTRITION NOTES

Per portion:

Energy	203Kcals/853kJ
Fat	10.52g
Saturated fat	2.05g
Cholesterol	0
Fiber	2.53g

1 Preheat the oven to 400°F. Lightly grease a 9 x 13in jelly roll pan and line it with nonstick parchment paper. Grease the paper.

2 For the roulade, place the egg whites in a large bowl and whisk them until they hold soft peaks. Gradually add the sugar, whisking hard between each addition.

3 Fold in the flour, orange rind and juice. Spoon the mixture into the prepared pan and spread it evenly.

4 Bake for about 15–18 minutes, or until the sponge is firm and light golden in color. Turn out on to a sheet of nonstick parchment paper and roll it up jelly roll-style loosely from one short side. Leave to cool.

5 For the filling, roughly chop the apricots, and place them in a saucepan with the orange juice. Cover the pan and leave to simmer for a few minutes until most of the liquid has been absorbed. Purée the apricots in a food processor or blender.

6 Unroll the roulade and spread with the apricot mixture. Roll up, then arrange strips of paper diagonally across the roll, sprinkle lightly with confectioner's sugar, remove the paper and scatter with orange zest to serve.

COOK'S TIP
Make and bake the sponge mixture a day in advance and keep it, rolled with the paper, in a cool place. Fill it with the fruit purée 2–3 hours before serving. The sponge can also be frozen for up to 2 months; thaw it at room temperature and fill it as above.

GREEK HONEY AND LEMON CAKE

INGREDIENTS

Makes 16 slices

3 tbsp sunflower margarine
4 tbsp clear honey
finely grated rind and juice of 1 lemon
⅔ cup skim milk
1¼ cups flour
1½ tsp baking powder
½ tsp grated nutmeg
¼ cup semolina flour
2 egg whites
2 tsp sesame seeds

1 Preheat the oven to 400°F. Lightly oil a 7½in square deep cake pan and line the base with nonstick baking paper.

2 Place the margarine and 3 tbsp of the honey in a saucepan and heat gently until melted. Reserve 1 tbsp lemon juice, then stir in the rest with the lemon rind and milk.

3 Sift together the flour, baking powder, and nutmeg, then beat in with the semolina. Whisk the egg whites until they form soft peaks, then fold evenly into the mixture.

4 Spoon into the pan and sprinkle with sesame seeds. Bake for 25–30 minutes, until golden brown. Mix the reserved honey and lemon juice and drizzle over the cake while warm. Cool in the pan, then cut into fingers to serve.

NUTRITION NOTES

Per portion:

Energy	82Kcals/342kJ
Fat	2.62g
Saturated fat	0.46g
Cholesterol	0.36mg
Fiber	0.41g

STRAWBERRY ROULADE

INGREDIENTS

Serves 6

4 egg whites
⅔ cup sugar
¾ cup flour
2 tbsp orange juice
1 cup strawberries, chopped
¾ cup low fat fromage frais
sugar, for sprinkling
strawberries, to decorate

1 Preheat the oven to 400°F. Oil a 9 x 13in jelly roll pan and line with nonstick baking paper.

2 Place the egg whites in a large bowl and whisk until they form soft peaks. Gradually whisk in the sugar. Fold in half of the sifted flour, then fold in the rest with the orange juice.

3 Spoon the mixture into the prepared pan, spreading evenly. Bake for 15-18 minutes, or until golden brown and firm to the touch.

4 Meanwhile, spread out a sheet of nonstick baking paper and sprinkle with sugar. Turn out the cake on to this and remove the lining paper. Roll up the cake loosely from one short side, with the paper inside. Cool.

5 Unroll and remove the paper. Stir the strawberries into the fromage frais and spread over the sponge. Reroll and serve decorated with strawberries.

NUTRITION NOTES

Per portion:

Energy	154Kcals/646kJ
Fat	0.24g
Saturated fat	0.05g
Cholesterol	0.25mg
Fiber	0.6g

SAGE SODA BREAD

This wonderful loaf, quite unlike bread made with yeast, has a velvety texture and a powerful sage aroma.

NUTRITION NOTES

Per loaf:

Energy	1251Kcals/5255kJ
Fat	9.23g
Saturated fat	2g
Cholesterol	7mg
Fiber	23.81g

INGREDIENTS

Makes 1 loaf

1½ cups whole-wheat flour
1 cup strong white flour
½ tsp salt
1 tsp baking soda
2 tbsp shredded fresh sage or 2 tsp dried sage
1¼–1¾ cups buttermilk

COOK'S TIP
As an alternative to the sage, try using either finely chopped rosemary or thyme.

1 Preheat the oven to 425°F. Sift the flours, salt and baking soda into a mixing bowl.

2 Stir in the sage and add enough buttermilk to make a soft dough.

3 Shape the dough into a round loaf with your hands and place on a lightly oiled cookie sheet.

4 Cut a deep cross in the top. Bake in the oven for about 40 minutes until the loaf is well risen and sounds hollow when tapped on the bottom. Leave to cool on a wire rack.

ZUCCHINI AND WALNUT LOAF

INGREDIENTS

Makes 1 loaf

3 eggs
½ cup light brown sugar
¼ cup sunflower oil
1½ cups whole-wheat flour
1 tsp baking powder
1 tsp baking soda
1 tsp ground cinnamon
½ tsp ground allspice
½ tbsp green cardamom pods, seeds
removed and crushed
1 cup coarsely grated zucchini
¼ cup walnuts, chopped
¼ cup sunflower seeds

NUTRITION NOTES

Per portion:

Energy	3073Kcals/12908kJ
Fat	201.98g
Saturated fat	26.43g
Cholesterol	654.5mg
Fiber	28.62g

1 Preheat the oven to 350°F. Grease the base and sides of a 2lb loaf pan and line with waxed paper.

2 Beat the eggs and sugar together and gradually add the oil.

3 Sift the flour into a bowl together with the baking powder, baking soda, cinnamon and allspice.

4 Mix into the egg mixture with the crushed cardamom, zucchini, walnuts and all but 1 tbsp of the sunflower seeds.

5 Spoon into the loaf pan, level off the top, and sprinkle with the remaining sunflower seeds.

6 Bake for about 1 hour or until a skewer inserted in the center comes out clean. Leave to cool slightly, then turn out on to a wire cooling rack.

SAFFRON FOCCACIA

A dazzling yellow bread with a distinctive flavor.

INGREDIENTS

Makes 1 loaf
pinch of saffron threads
⅔ cup boiling water
2 cups flour
½ tsp salt
1 tsp fast-rising dried yeast
1 tbsp olive oil

For the topping
2 garlic cloves, sliced
1 red onion, cut into thin wedges
rosemary sprigs
12 black olives, pitted and coarsely chopped
1 tbsp olive oil

NUTRITION NOTES

Per loaf:
Energy	1047Kcals/4399kJ
Fat	29.15g
Saturated fat	4.06g
Cholesterol	0
Fiber	9.48g

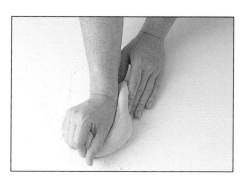

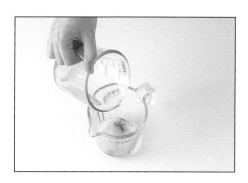

1 Place the saffron in a heatproof cup and pour on the boiling water. Leave to stand and infuse the saffron until lukewarm.

2 Place the flour, salt, yeast and olive oil in a food processor or blender. Gradually add the saffron and its liquid until the dough forms a ball.

3 Turn out on to a floured board and knead for 10–15 minutes. Place in a bowl, cover and leave to rise for about 30–40 minutes until doubled in size.

4 Punch down the risen dough on a lightly floured surface and roll out into an oval shape, ½in thick. Place on a lightly greased cookie sheet and leave to rise for 20–30 minutes.

5 Preheat the oven to 400°F. Use your fingers to press small indentations over the surface.

6 Cover with the topping ingredients, brush lightly with olive oil, and bake for about 25 minutes or until the loaf sounds hollow when tapped on the bottom. Leave to cool.

TOMATO BREADSTICKS

Once you've tried this simple recipe you'll never buy manufactured breadsticks again. Serve as a snack, or with aperitifs and a dip at the beginning of a meal.

--- INGREDIENTS ---

Makes 16
2 cups flour
½ tsp salt
½ tbsp fast-rising dried yeast
1 tsp clear honey
1 tsp olive oil
⅔ cup warm water
6 halves sun-dried tomatoes in olive oil, drained and chopped
1 tbsp skim milk
2 tsp poppy seeds

--- NUTRITION NOTES ---

Per portion:
Energy	82Kcals/346kJ
Fat	3.53g
Saturated fat	0.44g
Cholesterol	0
Fiber	0.44g

1 Place the flour, salt and yeast in a food processor or blender. Add the honey and olive oil and, with the machine running, gradually pour in the water (you may not need it all as flours vary). Stop adding water as soon as the dough starts to cling together. Process for 1 minute more.

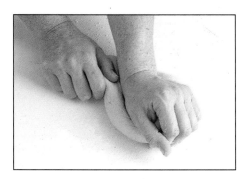

2 Turn out the dough on to a floured board and knead for 3–4 minutes until springy and smooth.

3 Knead in the chopped sun-dried tomatoes. Form into a ball and place in a lightly oiled bowl. Leave to rise for 5 minutes.

4 Preheat the oven to 300°F. Divide the dough into sixteen pieces and roll each piece into a 11 x ½in long stick. Place the sticks on a lightly oiled cookie sheet and leave to rise in a warm place for 15 minutes.

5 Brush the sticks with milk and sprinkle with poppy seeds. Bake for 30 minutes. Leave to cool on a wire cooling rack.

COOK'S TIP
Instead of sun-dried tomatoes, you could try making these breadsticks with reduced fat Cheddar cheese, sesame seeds or fresh chopped herbs.

CHERRY MARMALADE MUFFINS

INGREDIENTS

Makes 12

2 cups self-rising flour
1 tsp ground mixed spice
6 tbsp sugar
½ cup candied cherries, quartered
30ml/2 tbsp orange marmalade
⅔ cup skim milk
4 tbsp soft sunflower margarine
marmalade, to brush

1 Preheat the oven to 400°F. Lightly grease 12 deep muffin pans with oil.

2 Sift together the flour and spice, then stir in the sugar and cherries.

3 Mix the marmalade with the milk and beat into the dry ingredients with the margarine. Spoon into the greased pans. Bake for 20–25 minutes, until golden brown and firm.

4 Turn out on to a wire rack and brush the tops with warmed marmalade. Serve warm or cold.

NUTRITION NOTES

Per portion:

Energy	154Kcals/650kJ
Fat	3.66g
Saturated fat	0.68g
Cholesterol	0.54mg
Fiber	0.69g

DRIED FRUIT CAKE

INGREDIENTS

Makes 1 cake

¾ cup coarsely chopped mixed dried fruit, such as apples, apricots, prunes, and peaches
1 cup hot tea
2 cups whole-wheat self-rising flour
1 tsp grated nutmeg
4 tbsp brown sugar
3 tbsp sunflower oil
3 tbsp skim milk
raw sugar, to sprinkle

NUTRITION NOTES

Per cake:

Energy	1615Kcals/6786kJ
Fat	39.93g
Saturated fat	5.22g
Cholesterol	0.9mg
Fiber	31.12g

1 Soak the dried fruits in the tea for several hours or overnight. Drain and reserve the liquid.

2 Preheat the oven to 350°. Thoroughly grease a deep 7 in round cake pan and line the base with nonstick baking paper.

3 Sift the flour into a bowl with the nutmeg. Stir in the brown sugar, fruit, and tea. Add the oil and milk and mix well.

4 Spoon the mixture into the prepared pan and sprinkle with raw sugar. Bake for 50–55 minutes or until firm. Turn out and cool on a wire rack.

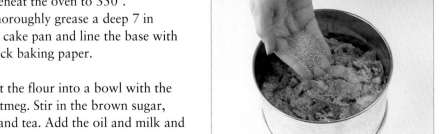

Banana Ginger Cake

This cake keeps well and really improves with keeping. Store it in a covered container for up to two months.

INGREDIENTS

Makes 1 cake
1¼ cups flour
2 tsp baking soda
2 tsp ground ginger
1¼ cups oatmeal
4 tbsp brown sugar
6 tbsp sunflower margarine
⅔ cup golden syrup
1 egg, beaten
3 ripe bananas, mashed
¾ cup confectioners' sugar
preserved ginger, to decorate

1 Preheat the oven to 325°F. Grease and line an 7 x 11in cake pan.

2 Sift together the flour, baking soda, and ginger, then stir in the oatmeal. Melt the sugar, margarine, and syrup in a saucepan, then stir into the flour mixture. Beat in the egg and mashed bananas.

3 Spoon into the pan and bake for about 1 hour, or until firm to the touch. Allow to cool in the pan, then turn out and cut into squares.

4 Sift the confectioners' sugar into a bowl and stir in just enough water to make a smooth, runny icing. Drizzle the icing over each square and top with a piece of preserved ginger, if you like.

> COOK'S TIP
> This is a nutritious, energy-giving cake that is a really good choice for lunch boxes as it doesn't break up too easily.

NUTRITION NOTES

Per cake:
Energy	3320Kcals/13946kJ
Fat	83.65g
Saturated fat	16.34g
Cholesterol	197.75mg
Fiber	20.69g

SPICED DATE AND WALNUT CAKE

A classic flavor combination, which makes a very easy low fat, high-fiber cake.

INGREDIENTS

Makes 1 cake
2½ cups whole-wheat self-rising flour
2 tsp mixed spice
¾ cup chopped dates
½ cup chopped walnuts
4 tbsp sunflower oil
½ cup brown sugar
1¼ cups skim milk
walnut halves, to decorate

1 Preheat the oven to 350°F. Grease and line a 2 lb loaf pan with non-stick baking paper.

2 Sift together the flour and spice, returning any bran from the strainer. Stir in the dates and walnuts.

3 Mix the oil, sugar, and milk, then stir evenly into the dry ingredients. Spoon into the prepared pan and arrange the walnut halves on top.

4 Bake the cake in the oven for about 45–50 minutes, or until golden brown and firm. Turn out the cake, remove the baking paper and leave to cool on a wire rack.

NUTRITION NOTES

Per cake:
Energy	2654Kcals/11146kJ
Fat	92.78g
Saturated fat	11.44g
Cholesterol	6mg
Fiber	35.1g

COOK'S TIP
Pecans can be used in place of the walnuts in this cake.

Sunflower-Raisin Scones

INGREDIENTS

Makes 10–12

2 cups self-rising flour
1 tsp baking powder
2 tbsp soft sunflower margarine
2 tbsp sugar
⅓ cup raisins
2 tbsp sunflower seeds
⅔ cup plain yogurt
about 2–3 tbsp skim milk

1 Preheat the oven to 450°F. Lightly oil a baking sheet. Sift the flour and baking powder into a bowl and rub in the margarine evenly.

2 Stir in the sugar, raisins, and half the sunflower seeds, then mix in the yogurt, with just enough milk to make a fairly soft, but not sticky dough.

3 Roll out on a lightly floured surface to about ¾ in thickness. Cut into 2½ in flower shapes or rounds with a cookie cutter and lift onto the baking sheet.

4 Brush with milk and sprinkle with the reserved sunflower seeds, then bake for 10–12 minutes, until puffed and golden brown.

5 Cool the scones on a wire rack. Serve split and spread with jam or low fat spread.

NUTRITION NOTES	
Per portion:	
Energy	176Kcals/742kJ
Fat	5.32g
Saturated fat	0.81g
Cholesterol	0.84mg
Fiber	1.26g

Prune and Candied Peel Buns

INGREDIENTS

Makes 12

2 cups flour
2 tsp baking powder
⅔ cup raw sugar
½ cup chopped dried prunes
⅓ cup chopped candied citrus peel
finely grated rind of 1 lemon
¼ cup sunflower oil
5 tbsp skim milk

NUTRITION NOTES	
Per portion:	
Energy	135Kcals/570kJ
Fat	3.35g
Saturated fat	0.44g
Cholesterol	0.13mg
Fiber	0.86g

1 Preheat the oven to 400°F. Lightly oil a large baking sheet. Sift together the flour and baking powder, then stir in the sugar, prunes, peel, and lemon rind.

2 Mix the oil and milk, then stir into the mixture, to make a dough which just binds together.

3 Spoon coarse mounds onto the baking sheet and bake for 20 minutes, until golden. Cool on a wire rack.

Banana-Orange Loaf

For the best banana flavor and a really good, moist texture, make sure the bananas are very ripe for this cake.

Makes 1 loaf

¾ cup whole-wheat flour
¾ cup flour
1 tsp baking powder
1 tsp ground mixed spice
3 tbsp slivered hazelnuts, toasted
2 large ripe bananas
1 egg
2 tbsp sunflower oil
2 tbsp clear honey
finely grated rind and juice 1 small
    orange
4 orange slices, halved
2 tsp confectioners' sugar

1 Preheat the oven to 350°F. Brush a 4 cup loaf pan with sunflower oil and line the base with nonstick baking paper.

2 Sift the flours with the baking powder and spice into a large bowl, adding any bran that is caught in the strainer. Stir the hazelnuts into the dry ingredients.

3 Peel and mash the bananas. Beat in the egg, oil, honey, and the orange rind and juice. Stir evenly into the dry ingredients.

4 Spoon into the prepared pan and smooth the top. Bake for 40–45 minutes, or until firm and golden brown. Turn out and cool on a wire rack to cool.

5 Sprinkle the orange slices with the confectioners' sugar and grill until golden. Use to decorate the cake.

> **Cook's Tip**
> If you plan to keep the loaf for more than three days, omit the orange slices, brush with honey, and sprinkle with flaked hazelnuts.

Nutrition Notes	
Per cake:	
Energy	1741Kcals/7314kJ
Fat	60.74g
Saturated fat	7.39g
Cholesterol	192.5mg
Fiber	19.72g

APRICOT YOGURT COOKIES

These soft cookies are very quick to make and are useful for the cookie jar or for lunch boxes.

―――――― INGREDIENTS ――――――

Makes 16
1½ cups flour
1 tsp baking powder
1 tsp ground cinnamon
1 cup oatmeal
½ cup brown sugar
½ cup chopped dried apricots
1 tbsp slivered hazelnuts or almonds
⅔ cup plain yogurt
3 tbsp sunflower oil
raw sugar, to sprinkle

1 Preheat the oven to 375°F. Lightly oil a large baking sheet.

2 Sift together the flour, baking powder, and cinnamon. Stir in the oatmeal, sugar, apricots, and nuts.

3 Beat together the yogurt and oil, then stir evenly into the mixture to make a firm dough. If necessary, add a little more yogurt.

4 Use your hands to roll the mixture into about 16 small balls, place on the baking sheet and flatten with a fork.

5 Sprinkle with raw sugar. Bake for 15–20 minutes, or until firm and golden brown. Leave to cool on a wire rack.

COOK'S TIP
These cookies do not keep well, so it is best to eat them within two days, or to freeze them. Pack into plastic bags and freeze for up to four months.

――――― NUTRITION NOTES ―――――

Per portion::
Energy	95Kcals/400kJ
Fat	2.66g
Saturated fat	0.37g
Cholesterol	0.3mg
Fiber	0.94g

EGGLESS CHRISTMAS CAKE

Makes one 7in square cake
⅔ *cup golden raisins*
⅔ *cup raisins*
½ *cup currants*
⅓ *cup candied cherries, halved*
¼ *cup cut candied peel*
1 cup apple juice
¼ *cup toasted hazelnuts*
2 tbsp pumpkin seeds
2 pieces preserved ginger in syrup,
  chopped
finely grated rind of 1 lemon
½ *cup skim milk*
¼ *cup sunflower oil*
1¾ *cups whole-wheat self-rising flour*
2 tsp cinnamon
3 tbsp brandy or dark rum
apricot jam, for brushing
candied fruits, to decorate

1 Place the golden raisins, raisins, currants, cherries, and peel in a bowl and stir in the apple juice. Cover and leave to soak overnight.

2 Preheat the oven to 300°F. Grease and line a 7in square cake pan.

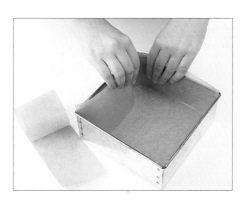

3 Add the hazelnuts, pumpkin seeds, ginger, and lemon rind to the soaked fruit. Stir in the milk and oil. Sift together the flour and spice, and stir into the mixture with the brandy or rum.

4 Spoon into the prepared pan and bake for about 1½ hours, or until the cake is golden brown and firm to the touch.

5 Turn out and cool on a wire rack. Brush with strained apricot jam and decorate with candied fruits.

NUTRITION NOTES

Per cake:

Energy	2702Kcals/11352kJ
Fat	73.61g
Saturated fat	10.69g
Cholesterol	2.4mg
Fiber	29.46g

CRANBERRY AND APPLE RING

Tangy cranberries add an unusual flavor to this low fat cake. It is best eaten very fresh.

INGREDIENTS

Makes 1 ring cake
2 *cups self-rising flour*
1 *tsp ground cinnamon*
½ *cup brown sugar*
1 *crisp eating apple, cored and diced*
⅔ *cup fresh or frozen cranberries*
4 *tbsp sunflower oil*
⅔ *cup apple juice*
cranberry jelly and apple slices, to decorate

1 Preheat the oven to 350°F. Lightly grease a 4 cup ring pan with oil.

2 Sift together the flour and ground cinnamon, then stir in the sugar.

3 Toss together the diced apple and cranberries. Stir into the dry ingredients, then add the oil and apple juice and beat well.

4 Spoon the mixture into the prepared ring pan and bake for about 35–40 minutes, or until the cake is firm to the touch. Turn out and leave to cool completely on a wire rack.

5 To serve, drizzle warmed cranberry jelly over the cake and decorate with apple slices.

COOK'S TIP
Fresh cranberries are available throughout the winter months and if you don't use them all at once, they can be frozen for up to a year.

NUTRITION NOTES

Per cake:
Energy	1616Kcals/6787kJ
Fat	47.34g
Saturated fat	6.14g
Cholesterol	0
Fiber	12.46g

CARROT CAKE WITH LEMON FROSTING

──── INGREDIENTS ────

Makes one 7in cake

1¾ cups whole-wheat self-rising flour

2 tsp ground allspice

⅔ cup brown sugar

3 medium carrots (about 1¾ cups), grated

⅓ cup golden raisins

5 tbsp sunflower oil

5 tbsp orange juice

5 tbsp skim milk

2 egg whites

For the frosting

¼ cup low fat cream cheese

finely grated rind of ½ lemon

2 tbsp clear honey

shreds of lemon rind, to decorate

1 Preheat the oven to 350°F. Grease a deep 7in round cake pan and line the base with nonstick baking paper.

2 Sift together the flour and spice, then stir in the sugar, carrots, and raisins. Mix the oil, orange juice, and milk, then stir into the dry ingredients. Whisk the egg whites until stiff, then fold in lightly and evenly.

3 Spoon into the pan and bake for 45–50 minutes, until firm and golden. Turn out and cool on a wire rack.

4 For the frosting, beat together the cheese, lemon rind, and honey until smooth. Spread over the top of the cooled cake, swirling with a metal spatula. Decorate the top with shreds of lemon rind.

──── NUTRITION NOTES ────

Per cake:

Energy	2182Kcals/9167kJ
Fat	61.79g
Saturated fat	8.37g
Cholesterol	3.25mg
Fiber	26.65g

CHEWY FRUIT GRANOLA SLICE

──── INGREDIENTS ────

Makes 8 slices

½ cup dried apricots, chopped

1 eating apple, cored and grated

1¼ cups Swiss-style granola (muesli)

⅔ cup apple juice

1 tbsp margarine

1 Preheat the oven to 375°F. Place all the ingredients in a large bowl and mix well.

2 Press the mixture into a 20cm/8in round, nonstick shallow pie pan and bake for 35–40 minutes, or until lightly browned and firm.

3 Score into wedges with a knife and leave to cool in the pan.

──── NUTRITION NOTES ────

Per portion::

Energy	112Kcals/467kJ
Fat	2.75g
Saturated fat	0.48g
Cholesterol	0.13mg
Fiber	2.09g

INDEX